HE COULD HAVE DONE ANYTHING

A Story About Serial Killers and the People Who Hunt Them

by Bob Druwing

ISBN 978-1-7327825-0-1 (print)
978-1-7327825-1-8 (ebook)

Front cover design by Todd Hebertson
Cover art by Chelsey Carpenter

Print and ebook layout by booknook.biz

To Joe Monaghan, who in 1967 insisted I begin keeping a journal.

1.

The Persistent Effects Of Choice

Paul Warren had always supposed that what he had been told while growing up was true, that he could have done anything in life, because he was very bright and talented, healthy and energetic and he came from fortunate circumstances, had loving parents and siblings, a middle-class family in a solid Midwestern community during good times, had been an outstanding student and athlete and had earned scholarships to more than one excellent college, but the choices he had made had led him to become one of the FBI's first "profilers" and from that time until now, in his third year of retirement, he believed *that* was what he was best at and, though it was no longer his profession, it was what he continued to be.

We all encounter chance, but Paul had always been certain that choices, bad ones and good ones, were the overriding determinants of where your life would go in the midst of an uncertain world and for whatever reasons that Paul had become passionately interested in puzzles, mysteries and human conflict as a boy, choosing to pursue those interests had determined the story of his life.

In the contemporary world, largely because of popular entertainment, most people thought of detective work in terms of forensics, but though forensics had, of course, played its part in his work and though he had earned his degree in law, Paul knew that his expertise was in abnormal psychology. Like all profilers, he had been a behavioral scientist.

2.

Homeostasis vs. Stim-Seeking Behavior

Though Paul had never sought a degree in psychology, he had studied it extensively and taught numerous courses in it and other subjects at the FBI Academy in Quantico, Virginia and would eventually be awarded an honorary doctorate in abnormal psychology from his alma mater, Notre Dame.

There were two concepts in the field of psychology that were never quite out of his mind. One was the idea of dividing behaviors into two basic groups: those that are motivated by the seeking of stimulation and those that are motivated by the desire to maintain homeostasis or lack of stimulation.

The other concept was something he had picked up in an undergraduate level psychology course called "The Nature Of Aggression." It was the idea, well borne out by statistical evidence, that the most reliable way to elicit an aggressive response from any organism was to block goal directed behavior of that organism.

At the moment Paul was leaning more towards homeostasis than stimulation, and this had been characteristic of his life since retirement, if not his lifelong psychological make-up. Right now he had just finished a delicious meal of his wife Joan's excellent roast duck with plum sauce and he was ready to settle in his favorite recliner, in his warm, oak panelled study, his favorite room in the house, and he wanted nothing more stimulating than a cup of good Sumatran coffee, while he watched the evening news in the peaceful company of Joan and their eight-year-old golden retriever, Rufrak.

It would seem this was too much to ask though, for the first item on the TV news concerned a Sparta, New Jersey woman who had gone missing in recent days and authorities now feared she had joined over a dozen women from the area who had vanished without a trace in the previous year, never to be seen again.

Paul knew they had another one of "them" out there. There was always another one of "them." They were predators, serial murderers, and at any given time it was estimated that there were around fifty of them at large and killing in the United States.

He almost wished that he hadn't begun drinking his coffee and sleep were still an option, but he (and Joan) knew that the gears in his mind had begun humming at the first mention of the missing woman and it wouldn't be possible to sleep now, coffee or no, until he'd once more juxtaposed everything he'd been learning about these women against literally everything else he knew.

"Have you spoken to Harvey about this woman?" asked Joan and immediately regretted mentioning Harvey Turner, who Paul had mentored since almost his first day in Quantico and who had risen to become one of the FBI's top profilers, because Rufrak, though reasonably docile like most golden retrievers, had an abnormal affection for Turner and had jumped up and begun to circle the room at the sound of his name and she knew he wouldn't forget it or be fully calmed again until the agent either showed up or something else that the dog held in very great esteem captured his attention.

Paul tried not to show, tried not to feel, any annoyance at his wife's indiscretion in juicing up the dog and said, "Not today."

3.

Down By The Old Mill Stream

Earlier that afternoon, a man dressed for trout fishing had carefully parked his van by where a stream crossed under a lightly trafficked road in a thickly forested section of Ogdensburg, New Jersey and stepped out into the rain that had been falling since shortly after dawn. Clearly, he had prepared for the rain, as he was wearing a Mossy Oak Camouflage rain poncho. In fact, he would only come here when it was raining.

Studiously surveying the landscape, he walked around the back of the van and to the sliding passenger side door, which was now fully invisible from the street side due to the vehicle's position in the proximate brush, slid open the door and pulled fishing gear and two heavy canvas bags from the vehicle, placing them on an overgrown pathway which led into the woods along the stream. He slid the door closed and stopped to listen.

He stood still for a full minute listening. All he heard was the rain and the stream and the birds. He walked around to the driver's side and stopped and looked up and down the road, first one way, eyes peeled, ears perked up, and then very slowly rotated his head until he had taken in everything that could be seen from where he stood. He always felt like he was being watched. This was partially the result of mental illness. He knew this and it was a constant struggle, under the circumstances, to distinguish between what was good and necessary caution and what was hallucinatory paranoia.

When he was sure he'd seen and heard nothing that seemed out of place, he relaxed a little and walked around to his gear and began to carry the bags containing Rachel Lutz into the woods.

4.

Tazer

Three days earlier Rachel Lutz had been a vivacious thirty seven-year-old married mother of three, who sold real estate part time, played the piano for her family and friends, kept a spotless home, baked German chocolate cakes that were actually raved about by their fortunate consumers and who didn't have one enemy anywhere on the planet.

She had purchased fresh eggs, butter and milk for one her famous cakes, from the organic market she frequented, and was at the rear of her car, when she saw that a man in a black sweat suit, who had parked his van next to the driver's side of her car, was now wrestling with what appeared to be a life-sized plush toy tiger in the cargo doorway of that van and there wasn't room for her to squeeze by and open her door. She was about to ask him to excuse her, but he looked up, saw her and profusely excused himself, backing into the van through the open cargo door, pulling his tiger in with him.

Rachel had thanked the man, taken her keys from her purse, slid one in the lock of her car door and turned it, when she felt a jolt from her head to her toes and in an instant she was looking up at the ceiling of the man's van. She was unable to move as she momentarily saw the man's face, flushed and wide-eyed, in place of the ceiling and then a chloroform soaked chamois cloth covered her face. She unwillingly gasped and inhaled deeply as the shock from the man's stun gun subsided and then everything was black.

5.

The Fisherman

The fisherman was a thirty-nine-year-old, unemployed, sometime deliveryman named Arlen Henniford, who hadn't done any actual fishing since he was a child. He hated fishing. It was one of the many things that fertilized the root of his problem.

Arlen's father had taught him to fish. Not his real father – he didn't know who his real father had been – but his mother's common-law husband, Joe Tuyers, who had insisted that Arlen refer to him as his father. Tuyers had brought him to the site of the old sawmill one Sunday morning shortly after he'd moved into the tiny house that Arlen had always lived in with his mother and had shown the boy all the finer points of trout fishing, from choosing bait to cleaning the catch.

That first morning of fishing had been enjoyable and Arlen thought that it was nice to finally have a father who took an interest in teaching him things like fishing. So what if he insisted on being referred to as your father, if he was going to play the role this well? Of all the men his tramp of a mother had brought home, this one was the first to stay longer than a weekend who hadn't ever hit him or even raised his voice.

They had worked their way a few hundred yards upstream and back and when they had returned to where the old mill had been, they sat on the remains of its stone foundation and had a lunch of bologna sandwiches and coffee from Tuyers' thermos. Arlen had never had coffee before. He thought it tasted strong and bitter. He didn't like it, but he didn't want to let Joe Tuyers know that.

Tuyers finished his sandwich and handed Arlen an apple. He polished another on the sleeve of his red flannel shirt and began to tell the boy that the old mill site had a legend. He said that he had heard the legend from his uncle, when he was a boy and his uncle had brought him there to fish. The sawmill was long since gone, even in those days. It seems that the old man who had lived there and run it, when Tuyers' uncle was a boy, had been suspected of molesting a local child and the townsfolk of Ogdensburg had promptly come to the mill one night and burned it to the ground, the old man along with it. His body had never been found!

Joe Tuyers excused himself, jumped down to the earthen floor of the depression that the stone foundation enclosed and, holding his apple in his teeth, moved a few feet away, pulled his hip-waders down against the tension of their suspender straps, unzipped his pants and relieved himself on the stone wall.

"You know what molesting means, boy?" he asked Arlen, as he stepped to the spot where he'd been sitting, took another bite from his apple and hefted himself back to a sitting position on the wall next to Arlen. He took the two last bites from his apple and tossed the core.

Still eating his own apple, Arlen replied, "Um, I guess I do," although he didn't.

"Oh yeah? What is it then?" Joe cackled down into the boy's face, spitting a tiny fleck of apple that flew into the open collar of Arlen's shirt and stuck to his skin.

"Well... um... well, I guess I'm not really sure...," said Arlen.

"Well... um... well, I guess you're not!" laughed Joe Tuyers and it was then that Arlen suddenly noticed that Tuyers hadn't put his business away after he had relieved himself and the confusion of how he could have overlooked such a thing, even in hip-waders, seemed to meld in Arlen's mind with the confusion of what happened next that he never clearly or completely remembered or really ever tried to.

He remembered cleaning fish afterward and that while sitting at a stoplight during the drive home, Tuyers had looked him in the eye very sternly and said, "Now I'm sure I don't have to tell you what might happen to you and your mother, should you tell anybody about our little secret."

After that day, Tuyers always treated him the same as he had previously. When they weren't on a fishing trip, he never laid a hand on the boy or showed any indication that he might be inclined to. They went fishing at the millstream every two or three weeks, when it was the season to and then it was the same as the first time, except that Tuyers would assault him immediately upon their arrival and then they would fish for hours, as if nothing odd had occurred, and return home.

When Arlen was twelve, Joe Tuyers was the first person he ever killed. He sliced the man's throat with a filleting knife as the moon hung in the sky and Arlen's mother, who was drunk and passed out, had lain in bed with the corpse for seven hours before she came to and screamed 'til they could hear her in Sparta.

They put her in a sanitarium.

Arlen they put in a home for wayward boys, where his treatment at the hands of others was soon worse than ever.

6.

All Over The News

In the morning, when Paul awoke, it was all over the news that every one of the missing North New Jersey area women had been found. Their apparent abductor had been found as well. Unfortunately, none of them had been found alive. And Paul knew that it was far too early to tell if all the missing women really had been found. This was media speculation.

According to the news, a private security guard had become suspicious, when he'd seen a van parked on the side of a lonely road while he was on his way to work and when it had still been there when he was returning home, he'd called the county sheriff who sent a deputy to investigate. By now clothing had been recovered with a dismembered body at the site in Ogdensburg, New Jersey that apparently matched what the most recent abductee, Rachel Lutz, had been wearing. There were thirteen skulls recovered in addition, the number of women who had gone missing under similar circumstances that authorities believed were being taken by the same person, and what appeared to be corresponding skeletal remains, but Paul knew of course that until autopsies were performed and matches confirmed that nothing about the identities of any of the remains could be said for certain.

They could in fact be more certain that the male body found at the site was the killer. It was evidently clear that he had been about to add his most recent prey to his "dumping grounds" when he had met with an accident. He had been ID'd as one Arlen Wesley Henniford of Ogdensburg.

Paul knew the name, remembered the case. He'd killed his step father, who'd been molesting him for years, when he was twelve years old. He'd been put "in the system", the catch-all term for youth services that could mean anything from the adoption system to incarceration. He couldn't quite remember the details with Henniford; it was a local case, not FBI; but it hardly mattered. As someone who had been sexually abused as a child, he fit the potential serial killer mold and having been anywhere in the system raised the chances of his wearing it. Paul knew that the other typical factors would be there.

Still it was all he could do to keep from calling Harvey Turner. He knew he'd be busy, either at the dump scene or the man's residence, trying to learn more as quickly as he could, just in case there was still an abductee alive. But it was so unusual to have found the man dead with his victims, and apparently of accidental causes, that he didn't know if he could wait until Turner next called him.

Of course, it wasn't unheard of. In the Houston case of Dean Corll in the early seventies, one of his young accomplices, Elmer Wayne Henley, had confessed to killing him when he'd had more than he could take of the torture murder game they and another young man, David Brooks, had been playing with their male, teenaged victims and his body had been recovered with those of the victims. Also there was an occasional suicide, like that of Jerome Anthony Anthony, whose body had been discovered by his employer hanging in the basement of his Santa Rosa, New Mexico home last year where the bodies of nine women were soon excavated from the dirt floor.

The more he thought about it though, Paul was at a loss to think of an example of a serial killer dying by accident in close proximity to his victims and that statistic alone made the thought keep popping into his head that if it seems too good to be true, it probably isn't true.

7.

Organized vs. Disorganized

Human beings are all the same in some ways and yet everyone is different from everyone else. Among serial killers, there are things that a profiler holds to be true about every last one of them. After that, the first division they make is between organized and disorganized killers and it's the very first thing that a professional profiler will be able to tell you based on observations of a crime scene or scenes. They're able to do this by drawing on what they have learned about patterns of behavior. They discern from the evidence what behaviors took place on the part of the criminal and from those behaviors they are able to judge with a reasonable degree of accuracy whether the killer was more methodical or more random, more calm or more frenzied, whether he had been more prepared for what he had done or less so, etc.

"Oh this guy was organized alright," said Harvey. He'd called Paul from his car en route from the Henniford house to the Lutz family home. "It's like he did *nothing* else. You've seen it before, Paulo." He'd started calling Paul "Paulo" after the older man had flown to Venice to marry Joan two and a half decades earlier and he'd come back a changed man. For a while, it was a running joke that Paul would quit the Bureau and go back to Italy to live the life of a bohemian artist and only Paul knew just how much his work alone had kept that from becoming the truth.

"So you're pretty sure he's the guy." said Paul.

"Paul, he tortured these women with fish hooks in a way I don't even want to describe and you don't want to hear. You've *never* seen anything quite like *this*, before. He lived alone in this place that looks from the outside like it's been un-lived in since he got put away as a child, but inside it's pretty clear what he's been doing. Yeah, we're not *pretty* sure, Paul, we're *sure*."

"He was living in his childhood home?" asked Paul incredulously.

"It seems his real father was some real estate tycoon. Made a king's ransom when the area went all millionaire vacation homes around the lake south of Sparta in the seventies or something. When he ran out on the kid and his mom, he was damn financially responsible about it, I'll tell you that. The house was paid for and the size of the trust fund was enormous for those days, but structured in such a way that nobody could have bought a pleasure boat. Henniford was living on that and may not even have had any appreciation of how rich he was. The property was maintained empty all the years he was away. Still looks it except for this guy's carnage. The mother died in the hospital. Never came back. I'm hoping to interview the former caretaker after I see Mr. Lutz again."

"Accidental," Paul said one more time.

"He was using the foundation stones from an old mill to conceal their shallow graves, tipping over sections of wall. A whole section of wall collapsed on him, Paul. The good Lord did it, or he did it to himself by being in the right place at the right time. That's as far as we can move from accidental on this one."

"Thanks, Harv."

"Sure. Pet Rufrak for me, wouldja? And say 'hi' to Joan. I'm nearly there, Paul; gotta go."

"You bet, Harvey."

And that was that. It was surely unusual, but like the saying says, there's a first time for everything. He'd let it rest. After all, it wasn't really his business anymore, was it?

8.

The Dream

The dream had come less frequently since he had retired, but now he was having it again.

In the dream, Paul was standing in the hallway of the court-house in Las Vegas, Nevada with Harvey Turner and Mrs. Thomas McAdams, Shirley, the mother of a murdered girl, whose killer, one Andrew Travis Johansen, had just been released on a technicality at his trial. He was a sexual predator and serial killer and everyone knew it.

He was the type that didn't even try to hide his pride in his accomplishments, but would sit in the courtroom day after day with a gloating grin on his face and Paul knew he was reliving his abduction, sexual torture and murder of Heidi Anne McAdams, Tom and Shirley's perfect daughter, as their details were being revealed by the prosecutor. She'd been an A student, studied ballet, played piano and the flute and was the spitting image of a six-teen-year-old Reese Witherspoon. She had been her parents' only offspring and other than a childhood bout with rheumatic fever, they had never had anything that could have been called a problem with her.

There had been at least four other young female victims, but not enough evidence to bring charges against Johansen except in the McAdams case and now his lawyer had somehow gotten his hands on the video tape of his arrest from the dashboard camera of the Nevada State Trooper who had pulled him over on the night of the McAdams abduction and shown that he had intentionally confessed that her body was in the trunk, after he'd been arrested for driving drunk, but before he'd been Mirandized.

Now the judge had decided that he not only must be freed, but every thread of evidence they had on him had come subsequently and it was now all considered to be "fruit of the poison tree." They had nothing on which to hold him and they might never have.

Just as it had been on that swelteringly hot day four years ago, the air conditioning wasn't working in the dream and Shirley McAdams, who had kept her husband on just this side of sanity since their daughter had been taken, looked like she might faint. The McAdamses' best friends, Phillip Smithson, the Senator's son who had made good on his own, first as an outstanding college and professional athlete and then as a sportscaster and creator of The Gaming Broadcast Corporation, and his wife Andrea, were there now insisting she have a seat on a nearby bench. Where was Tom McAdams anyhow? Oh, yes, he had excused himself and gone to the restroom. Paul had assumed he needed to be alone for a moment to be sick.

And now there was a commotion in the mass of people behind him in the hall, reporters mostly. Apparently the paperwork had been completed and Andrew Travis Johansen was about to join them in the hallway. Paul was suddenly terrified and he knew he knew why and knew just as clearly that he wouldn't be able to do anything about the reason why, because somehow whatever it was had already happened. He began to turn toward the commotion and he felt like his body was made of ice. He felt frozen and as he struggled to move, he thought his body would shatter from the stress he was exerting on it. He tried to force himself to move and he found himself awake in a cold sweat.

"Is it that dream?" he heard Joan ask him in the darkness and he felt her arm enclose him and her body pull close as she spooned with him. She placed her right leg over his legs.

"Yeah," he said, deeply exhaling, and he reached with his left hand to grasp her right forearm. "It's okay, Joanie. Go back to sleep."

She held him tight and he knew that she was trying to make him feel that everything really was okay.

9.

Prediction

"The usefulness of any theory, the accuracy of the theory itself, its acceptability as a theory, comes in its ability to allow us to use it to predict future events," explained Harvey Turner to his partner, Jim Ascuto, as they walked to a morning briefing at FBI headquarters, "and in chess, the greatest masters are the ones who can see the highest number of moves ahead. The thing about Warren is he could walk into a crime scene and inside of a few minutes he could entirely deconstruct it in reverse time in his mind and tell you *exactly* what had happened and predict most of the characteristics of the person responsible."

"Uh-huh." Ascuto had heard this before, of course. Warren was legendary. Jim had even taken a course from him at Quantico, but he'd never worked with him.

"Sure, this is what we *do*! But with Paul it was really amazing. It was like having somebody walk up to a chessboard with a completed checkmate on it and having them tell you every single move that had been made, because they had the ability to imagine the entire match in reverse. He was really the best that's ever been!"

Ascuto did not respond. He knew that what he had just heard was somehow related to what he was about to hear. Turner was just warming up. They had come to the small conference room now and the senior agent entered first to begin his briefing.

When Joan arrived in her kitchen she was surprised not to find her husband. On nights when he had the dream, he had always had difficulty sleeping afterwards and he'd rise early and she'd generally find him enjoying coffee and the morning paper at the dining table, having made breakfast for them both and having consumed his. In the year before he retired, she would otherwise find him either painting or drawing in pen and ink, out in his studio, which Paul had converted from one bay of what had been a two car garage, so she proceeded across the room, through the dining room and out the French doors leading to their back yard.

She found him there, sitting at his drawing table, which was yet another surprise, because he had only produced watercolors since his retirement, had done no drawing whatsoever since he had stopped working on cases. It was a thing that went hand in hand with working on a case. He'd begin a pen and ink drawing after he had started a new case. His work was very detailed. He'd draw one thin line in black ink on his white paper, usually very short, usually completely straight, then another elsewhere and on and on. He worked slowly and carefully, but appeared to be completely relaxed at his work. The thing that Joan found completely astounding was that she never could see anything at all evolving in the picture until it was almost complete and suddenly it would be done: the most magnificent rendering of a landscape you could possibly imagine!

Apparently this was going to be a morning for exceptions, for as she looked past him at the large sheet of paper carefully taped to his drawing board, she could see that it had not one line on it.

He heard her enter and turned to meet her eyes.

"Artist's block?" she asked. "I thought you'd be painting." It was a lie, wishful thinking really. He had never painted when he was working on a case and she knew, reluctantly, that he was now working on one.

He Could Have Done Anything

He looked up at her with what she judged to be somewhat of a sly sort of grin and asked, "Want to go to Santa Fe in a couple of days?"

10.

Scientific Method

The scientific method, a process used by every scientist, can be broken down into the steps of asking a question concerning what it is you want to know, doing research or gathering information about what you want to know, formulating a hypothesis or making an "educated guess" about the answer to your question, conducting a precise experiment designed to accurately test your hypothesis, collecting data from your experiment, analyzing your data and drawing a conclusion about the correctness or incorrectness of your hypothesis.

"Ogdensburg!?" exclaimed Harvey into his phone, later that morning. "Well, sure there's no problem authorizing you to go on the site, Paulo, but it's all torn apart now, of course; you'd learn much more from the first photos…"

"Yeah, I was hoping you'd bring those by Sunday, but Joanie and I are thinking of flying to Sante Fe now on Friday, so now I'm hoping you could email them to me here in the car. I'm already on my way." In fact he'd been driving for over an hour. It would take perhaps another two to get to Ogdensburg from Paul's home in the Virginia countryside.

"Well, sure, but the question is why, Paul. Henniford's the right guy and there's only one vic left who we're not positive on the ID and we're pretty sure about her."

"I have a bigger question, Harv. Just doing a little research."

"You gonna tell me the question?" Harvey knew the man well enough to know he'd have told him already, if he'd intended to.

"If you can be patient and I see what I expect to in Ogdensburg, I may even have a hypothesis for you tonight."

"Expect to see! What is it you *expect* to see?" asked Harvey.

"Potential."

"Aaaaah. You want to see the house, too?"

"Nah, it's not relevant," Paul answered.

"Not relevant." Harvey tried to digest that idea.

"Oh, Harv, wha'd the coroner finally say 'bout cause of death on Henniford?"

"Well the guy was crushed by some pretty massive stones, so it's kinda take your pick, but his conclusion was massive head trauma, but if it hadn't've been that, it would've been something else resulting from being crushed, like internal organ failure… The guy was flattened!"

"Massive head trauma. Okay. So I'll call you later from home or New Bedford."

"Massachusetts?" Harvey was now truly mystified. "Why New Bedford?"

"Depending on what I see in New Jersey, there's a man I might want to see there."

"You had the dream again," said Harvey.

"You know me too well, Harv. I had it last night *and* the night before. That has *never* happened before," Paul stressed.

"Paulo, I don't know quite how to say this, but we've been very good friends for a long time so I'll just say it."

When silence followed, Paul said, "But you're not saying anything, Harvey."

"Regardless of the dream, I think you're bored. Not like you miss this job or anything; that's not what I'm saying; but if I didn't know you better, I'd say you're feeling compelled to solve a puzzle, when the only puzzle is *why* you have this dream and it was a *very* traumatic experience, Paulo; the real mystery is why I don't have nightmares about it!"

"You're maybe right about that last part, Harv. Send those pictures, would you, and I'll talk to you later," said Paul and he hung up.

11.

Headhunters

Dennie Bordeaux had a self-made sign on his bedroom wall, just above and behind his computer monitor, which read: "Among Headhunters The Man Who Refuses To Hunt Humans Is Dysfunctional."

He figured everything is relative, a matter of value judgments. He understood that most people don't see it that way, but he also understood that he was *way* smarter than most people. Assholes.

Dennie lived with his mother, "the fat shit", in Buxton, Maine and wondered how such a stupid woman could have such an intelligent son. He figured his dad must have been a genius before the accident on the black ice one winter night on Rte. 95 and the lengthy coma that preceded his death, when Dennie was only seven.

His mother didn't seem to have any idea what to do, during the almost three years that Dennie's father lay dying. "What'll we do, Dennie? I just don't know what we'll ever do," he could remember her saying and it seemed the only thing that had changed about her since his father died was that she'd gotten older and fatter.

She had made him work at McDonald's over in Scarborough, until he got fired for calling a girl a whore after she'd addressed him as "Pizza-face", which was pretty stupid, because she *was* a whore and everyone knew it! Assholes! When he was in high school she'd been the biggest whore in school, for Chrisake! Man, that still pissed him off and it had been what? Almost five years!

He didn't need the money. His mother gave him whatever he wanted. She'd just made him work there, because he wasn't doing anything after he graduated and she'd said that wasn't right. What did she know? He could make money any time he wanted, even in this backward place. Besides, he was doing plenty. He had plans. He was going to write something that would make him famous. Either that or go to Hollywood and become an actor. Maybe even both!

But for now he was biding his time. For now he was smoking weed and taking x or acid (it really *was* mind-expanding) once in a while and customizing his badass pickup truck (there were always minor adjustments to be made when your objective was to attract "the little birds" and at the same time have the vehicle go unremembered by any would-be witnesses) and headhunting.

Buxton was a good place to live, if you wanted to headhunt. To begin with, there was really nothing to do in the whole fucking state of Maine, so all the kids were bored and looking for some excitement. Because of Buxton's location, he had his choice of great places to headhunt. He could drive into nearby Portland, where it was always relatively busy, or up to Sebago Lake or out to the shore, where in summertime the tourist girls were always ripe and plentiful. Little assholes! Ha ha! He loved the double entendre in that!

But his favorite way to headhunt was just to take Rte. 4 to Rte. 5 and then cruise north, sometimes all the way to Rangeley and back, just listening to the tunes at a reasonable level and doing the doobs and looking normal, while he waited for a little bird to give itself up to him. That's what they did, even the ones on vacation, they were so bored.

They'd see him, he'd make eye contact and in a split second, without a word, they said, "Take me; I'm yours." He'd pull up and say, "You like my truck?" and before you could take a photograph, they'd be happy to accept his invitation to go for a ride to wherever and never come back.

That's the way he had decided to go this morning after his mother had pissed him off asking him if he had eaten the last piece of blueberry pie. Asshole! Who the fuck do you think ate it, if you didn't, you fat shit! He'd only traveled about five miles and now he was passing the new supermarket in East Waterboro and oh my god this was gonna be too easy! Look at that little blonde bird on the side the road. Is she actually hitch-hiking? Yes, she is! Look at those tiny white short shorts and those itty-bitty titties! Here little birdie, birdie. Here little birdie.

He pulled over next to her and she smiled in the passenger side window. "I'm just going up to Little Ossipee Pond," she said. She was wearing braces. He hated braces. She looked like she was maybe fourteen, tops.

"No problema, senorita! Climb in," said Dennie.

She took a little whiff of the scent of marijuana in the cab, her smile grew wider and she opened the door and climbed in.

12.

Potential

The Ogdensburg site was still being processed, of course, would go on being processed for a good long while. In fact there were so many graves, *most* of the bodies had not been removed. If Henniford hadn't left the dead women's clothing and other belongings with their bodies, they'd never have been able to get so many preliminary ID's so quickly. However, it was fortunate that they had been looking for all of these women to begin with, so it was a matter of matching remains to known identities. Too often they were left with victims who remained Jane and John Does.

This processing was what Turner had meant by "all torn apart." They preferred to see a scene that was as fresh as possible, before *anyone* had changed anything. Paul spoke with a deputy sheriff posted as security out on the road and, as luck would have it, he was the one who'd found the site. He'd done everyone a favor by literally backing out of the scene in his own footprints. It was an outstanding observation of correct procedure for preservation of evidence. Paul hoped he'd be rewarded for it and told him so. It turned out he already had been. He had requested his current duty.

Paul's first instinct was to walk the entire perimeter of the yellow tape, but he resisted and made his way up the path along the stream the several hundred yards to the mill site. He had a few words with a couple of the forensic techs, who were concentrating like archeologists on their tasks, mainly to let them know who he was. They told him they'd been expecting him and impulsively rattled off the "Cliff Notes" version of what they knew.

Paul thanked them, clarified exactly where Henniford had been found and inspected that area thoroughly, then he walked the perimeter of what remained of the mill's foundation, surveying the surroundings and stopping to examine the wall along most of the places where it remained intact, which were many. Twice he climbed down to the floor and closely perused what remained of the corroded mortar between the large stones. It appeared the mill had covered quite an expanse, in its day.

When he got back to the path, he threw the techs a wave and went on his way. He thought about the circumference of the entire site again, but once more, decided against walking it, stopped briefly and asked the deputy what the weather had been like in the hours before he was called to investigate Henniford's van, got in his car and drove off to New Bedford.

13.

Concentric Circles

"The law's a pain in the ass, Paul. Decisions to prosecute or not being made based upon whether reasonable doubt about guilt might be shown at trial… Where's the science, hmm? Every D.A. since Pina has sworn they were gonna solve this case and here we are, after twenty years, with lugatz!" exclaimed Dr. Terrance Davis, Bristol County's workaholic coroner. When Paul had called the night before, Davis had asked him to come by the house in one of New Bedford's nicer sections. He was on a rare vacation and there wasn't so much to catch up on around the house that he couldn't spend some time filling Paul in and taking him to see what he wanted to see.

They were old friends. They'd met at a forensics conference in 1976. There had been a cocktail party after the orientation ceremonies on the first night of the conference and just when things were about as festive as they were going to get, Davis happened to be strolling past a group of folks to whom he overheard Paul saying, "Of course, we *know* Oswald was the lone assassin."

Maybe it was the tone of voice, maybe it was the alcohol; Davis liked to believe it was because they were in the same circle of scientists; he stopped and said, "Excuse me. My name is Dr. Terrance Davis and I don't know who you are or what your expertise may be, but I have to tell you, my friend, that you've been misinformed, at best."

Paul introduced himself and quickly explained that he was being sarcastic with his Oswald comment and soon they were exchanging their favorite discrepancies in the Warren Commission's case. Now, over thirty years later, as the people who shared most of Paul's interests could be placed in tighter and tighter circles, Davis was among those closest to the center. The doctor refused to retire and since Doris Davis's passing on of breast cancer in '99, he had lived for his four kids, nine grandchildren, a few close relationships and the work. The men enjoyed coffee and some delicious pastry from a little, local, Portuguese bakery, as they got updated.

"Well, here's the thing, Terry. From my reading of this – and I was on the net last night refreshing my memory – Pina said, in 1990, that he had it narrowed down to one *definite* suspect…"

"Before he was voted out of office."

"Right. Straight up, do you know if he believed it was DeStefano?"

"He didn't believe it was DeStefano."

"Okay. That's what I'd figured. And Pimental, the O.D., it was an O.D., but accidental, suicide, what?"

"Well, I'll say this, Paul: the guy had enough cocaine in him to kill four guys his size. So he may have snorted a lot more than he was used to, or the purity was exceptional, right? Well, tests on the powder at the scene showed positive for nearly pure coke. My finding was accidental overdose. Happens every day."

"Okay and the police were never able to get anything on who he was with that last night?" asked Paul.

"Not sure there was anybody at the end and as for earlier, there were just rumors. There was a rolled up twenty still lying there he'd been snorting with. Would another coke-head have left that?"

"Yeah, but where does a guy who's arrested only months before for stealing food get the money for enough pure coke, all at once, to send four junkies to their maker? He'd fallen a long way since his days as a practicing attorney, Terry. I'm sure he had a lot of dirty connections from here to Florida once, but if he had the resources to be connected to anything coming in off a boat, uncut, would he be squatting in an abandoned building?"

Davis nodded at the logic of that. "He was a scumbag all along, Paul. You know about those movies with the dog, right? Whether or not he killed eleven prostitutes, he was a scumbag."

"Well, let's go see his place then, shall we?"

14.

Condemned

Kevin Pimental had indeed fallen quite a distance since occupying a sprawling home in the best part of town, fallen all the way to a decaying triple decker in the worst part of town, where, in a first floor kitchen in the rear of the house, which Paul now viewed in the glow of a powerful flashlight, he had taken his last breath. That had been the previous Autumn, but little had changed in this old building, which was now scheduled for the wrecker.

Pimental had never denied having an intimate relationship with Martine DeSimone, one of the dead women, or that he had provided legal representation for several more. He'd even been charged with DeSimone's murder briefly in 1990, but a grand jury had decided there was insufficient evidence to try him and those charges were dropped. The driveway and patio of the home where he'd lived with DeSimone had been torn up last May, in a new search for "DNA and fiber evidence", courtesy of the newly elected district attorney, whose spokesman explained to the press that new technologies were available now which might shed some light on the cold but well remembered case and bring some closure to both the victims' families and the community at large.

Nothing came of it.

Paul examined the death scene, then the remainder of the first floor apartment. The front stairs were in disrepair and impassible, but he left Davis behind on the rear porch, urging him to rest his knees, while be made his way up the back stairway and briefly scoped out the two upper vacant apartments. He was about to return, but then he paused and instead climbed the stairs to the roof access door, which hung open on its one remaining lower hinge.

He stepped out onto the roof and did a 360 of the neighborhood, as he walked the roof's perimeter, occasionally peering down at the closer surroundings, returned to the door and was soon again in the doctor's company examining the basement.

"This is a dead neighborhood, Terry," he said when they were back in Paul's car.

"You bet. If the city hadn't been nailing up plywood and a condemned sign on every building on the street that morning, hell, he might still be in there."

15.

The Funnel

Where the Pendexter Brook crosses under Cramm Rd. in Parsonsfield and again further south where it crosses under Stone Hill Rd. in Limerick, it looks like just another trout stream, except during the snow melt and extremely rainy times and the same can be said of the Federson Brook, which runs beneath Cramm Rd. a short distance east of the Pendexter, so one would never suspect without having observed it, that approximately half way between Cramm Rd. and Stone Hill Rd., more than a mile deep in the woods from any paved road, where the Federson became a tributary of the Pendexter, they both looked like rivers and were at least twenty yards wide. If one followed Owls Hill Rd. until the pavement ran out and then continued into the woods on the dirt road, eventually this fork in the waterways was reached. Since men had been coming here, it had been obvious to them that this was a perfect hunting area, as it was a natural trap where a clever hunter could funnel his prey into the confluence of the two brooks, leaving it no chance of escape other than to brave the water or turn back toward its pursuer. Indeed the remains of several hunting camps could be detected in the immediate area.

On one of his many re-con missions, four-wheeling up innumerable dirt roads in Maine and New Hampshire, Dennie Bordeaux had also found a cliff at the top of Cole's Hill, a few miles northeast of this spot, with similar potential for cornering a little bird, but what if she jumped? It wouldn't be wise to leave her there.

No way. That's definitely against the rules. He had rules. He'd studied all the great ones, that truck driver, what was his name? O'Donnell? O'Connell? O'Connor? Whatever. Jesperson. And Bundy! Bundy was his hero. Bundy was a headhunter! They had rules for themselves and they followed them. He took *their* rules and combined and refined 'em and yeah, no way. He'd have to climb down and around the hill… forget it! So he'd brought her here to play the game. It was the closest place anyhow and he hadn't used it yet. You didn't use anywhere twice.

That was an unbreakable rule.

Stephanie had never been so scared in her life. He'd hit her in the solar plexus as soon as she'd closed the truck door, knocking the wind out of her. Then he'd grabbed her by the hair and twisted her around and down, forcing her to the floor. He'd ordered her to get down and stay down and not make a sound unless asked to or, he'd promised, he was going to hurt her really, really bad. Then he'd let her hair go and quickly pulled a strip of dark green duct tape from the dashboard and clamped it over her mouth. He'd looked her in the eye until she was afraid he would crash the truck – but then maybe she could get away! – and said, "I'll kill you, if you don't do everything I tell you to do, when I tell you to do it."

She had done as she was told to. She had gotten out of the truck and taken all her clothes off, when told to. When he'd stood there looking at her body, she knew he was trying to embarrass her and it made her *very* angry inside. When he'd told her not to try to hide herself with her arms or hands, she'd done what she was told to do. Then, when he'd bound her wrists with a single plastic flex-cuff and took off the duct tape, so she could use her mouth, she'd made up her mind right then that she would bite him, when he was at his weakest, and run like jack rabbit, but he had held a huge, black machete, that looked like something from Tim Burton's *Planet Of*

The Apes, to her throat and now, as she was gathering all her courage, he stopped her and pushed her away at arms length and said, "Hey, you know what?"

He grabbed her wrists and stood her up and, in a stroke, he cut the flex-cuff from her wrists, pocketed it, then fastened his pants. This was his favorite part. He loved to see the surprise and relief and then the shock and disappointment and finally the terror, deeper than ever, when he said, "I think, since you've been so obedient, I'm just going to let you go now," and he pointed with his machete up the road and looked, not in the direction they had come, but the other way, to where the road became little more than a trail before ending at the brookside, "but you'd better run," he said and turned his head back anticipating that delightful look of pure fear and… it wasn't there! And neither was she!

At the sound of the word "go" Stephanie had taken off like a hundred meter sprinter out of the blocks and by the time Dennie's head had completed its turning, she was thirty of those meters away and gaining speed, as she approached a gradual incline. He figured the hill would slow her right down, as he jumped and set after her, but he'd hardly taken three steps when, what luck!, he saw her turn right at the base of the hill and head west toward the Pendexter Brook! He quickly returned to the truck and got his blow gun, then bolted up the road, confident he could head her off. After all, he'd been training for this.

16.

Priority One

When Paul called Harvey Turner, he discovered he couldn't be reached short of an emergency except on bureau business, because the agent was in the air, en route to the Sanford Regional Airport in Sanford, Maine. Five girls in their early to mid-teens and one woman who was twenty-two, but who fit the physical characteristics of the others, 4'9" to 5'2", 87 to 105 lbs., had disappeared right off the streets of Southern Maine in the past fourteen months and now another petite, sixteen-year-old girl from West Roxbury, Massachusetts, one Stephanie Daley, who had been spending two weeks at her Uncle Peter and Aunt Marie's summer place on Little Ossipee Pond in Waterboro, was nowhere to be found.

Having only been missing for six hours (confirmed by a Dunkin' Donuts' security camera), she ordinarily wouldn't have even been considered missing by authorities, but she fit perfectly into the M.O. of someone they were already looking for and if she was taken by him, she was now the third to be snatched in York County, the same York County that held Kennebunkport and the George and Barbara Bush compound. The first broadcasts had barely come over the police radios, when the phone rang in the Director's office and finding Stephanie Daley and her abductor suddenly became FBI priority number one and Turner was on a plane within the hour.

Paul's first urge was to get in his car and drive four hours north to Waterboro, but it didn't fit his agenda and, of course, it wasn't his job. He wasn't going anywhere tonight. Davis had cracked open a bottle of twelve-year-old scotch, when they'd returned from a dinner at The Catch O' The Day, a dinner Paul insisted on and Terry was reluctant to accept, preferring always to cook for friends, and it had been too long since Paul had had a chance to sit and talk with his friend over a glass of good whiskey, so he stuck with the original plan of spending the night at Davis's and driving home in the morning, after the commuter traffic rush had subsided.

"That one sounds like a bitch, sport." Terry had a tendency to call you "sport" after a couple drinks, if he liked you and to use "buddy", if he had his doubts; "pal" had resulted in more than one scuffle with people he clearly hadn't cared for. "No remains?"

"Femur from the older one, found by a hunter in North Jesus or something. Dolly Mountain. Byron's the town. The Swift River. Dolly Mountain… don't know if that means anything. But she's the one he took from Portland, on a busy Saturday night. It's two hours plus, from where the bone was found."

"Big comfort zone," commented the doctor.

"Big comfort zone," Paul agreed. "In the most heavily forested state in the nation. Did you know that? No? Yeah, the whole state's like one big forest, so…"

"So they got their work cut out for them."

"Yeah, they do," said Paul. "On the other hand, if this is a third one now in the same county, with the other four and the location of the one find to plot, the grid on this guy must be looking fairly promising."

"You'd think," agreed Terry.

17.

The Grid

The grid was looking promising to Harvey Turner. With the location of the latest abduction approximated and plotted into the computer program that would now do the work that used to require a map and push-pins, with their corresponding concentric circles representing degrees of probability of your perp living or working within them, he could be fairly certain that their current perp was based in one of four towns that met on the boarder of York and Cumberland counties: Standish, Gorham, Hollis and Buxton. He knew this much from his laptop.

When he reached the mobile base in the large motor home, in the parking lot of the new Fine Brother's supermarket, he learned that local agents had moved on to analysis of the traffic on Rte. 5, digital recordings from the supermarket's and the adjacent Dunkin Donuts' security camera systems, following Stephanie's departure from the parking lot, while local authorities had organized a host of volunteers into specific searches. They'd gathered a great deal of data on vehicles. Unfortunately the license plates on all traffic passing in both directions and not entering or having exited the parking lot were altogether invisible, but the computers were running the plates they could see for registered owners and automatically cross-referencing them with known sex offenders and various other high-risk probability data bases.

If I can just make it to the water, thought Stephanie, I'll get away from this sick piece of shit rat bastard! She'd seen the glint of the setting sun on what appeared to be a river through the trees as soon as she'd looked around, when they'd first arrived and what she could see to the north and west appeared to be a flood plain, thick with vegetation, much like what she was used to seeing along the Charles River at home.

Stephanie had glanced back at him in the instant after she'd hooked a right off the dirt road and saw him freeze and turn back toward his truck. All she knew was that it would buy her a little more time, but was he going back for the truck? Would he head her off, even if she got to the water? No time to worry about it. Just run. She ran. Dennie Bordeaux didn't know he was dealing with a star athlete. Stephanie had lettered in cross country, track & field and swimming at her high school, since her sophomore year. She'd hardly been out of Little Ossipee Pond in a week.

Dennie Bordeaux made it to the top of the grade and ran a good fifty yards more on the road, before coming to a path on his right that he knew well. It led all the way to the Pendexter and as he ran along it, he figured as he reached the western edge of the hill, he'd spot her coming upon the scraggly brush of the flood plain. From there she'd clearly see that even if she took one of the few trails through it, it would only lead to the water that was visible beyond it and probably opt to follow the curvature of the hill and come right to him. The area had been logged six years earlier and there were stumps, bad logs, dead branches and holes everywhere. Plenty of places to hide. Would she hide? No, she'll run. He was sure of it.

As he came to the edge of the hill, he slowed and scanned the hillside and flood plain. Now... where is that little bird? He froze and crouched, peering intently as far around the hill as he could see. He tried to calmly catch his breath, as he rotated his gaze counter-clockwise and took a step down the slope. Wait! What is that, a splash? Right there! Oh Christ, she's in the water and she's swimming south!

He slid on the leaf covered ground, as he whipped around, almost dropping his blow-gun, and began sprinting back to his truck. A few hundred yards north of Stone Hill Rd. was a foot-bridge. He thought of that bridge now and was sure he could take the road south to a path the ski-mobilers used, which led right to that bridge and, if he recalled correctly, the path was even wide enough for him to drive most of the way, maybe all of the way, to the bridge. How fast could she swim? Where exactly did the brook become too shallow and rocky to actually swim? He probably had time to spare. Still, the sun was going down. It would be dark within the hour.

18.

The Power Of The Subconscious Mind

"You know how he is, Ma," explained Jeff Warren to his mother. "It's all about the failure of the super-ego, the lack of a conscience in these people. He has complete faith that very thing will always put them at a disadvantage, while at the same time he has faith in is own subconscious. What's that thing he always says about dreams? 'We don't think we understand what we haven't put…' "

"We tend to believe we can't understand what we can't verbalize, but the subconscious uses dreams every night to sort things out in symbols," Joan quoted her husband.

"That's it. And the other thing he likes to say, 'a hunch is as good as a reason,' it's all a product of having absolute faith in his powers of observation and the ability of his *entire* mind to sort things out. *I've* got a hunch that, in the long run, this dream is gonna prove to be a good thing."

"Well, I wish it would hurry the hell up. He had it two nights in a row. He thinks I didn't notice the night before last when the Lutz woman was taken. He's never had it two nights in a row before, as far as I know, and it bothers me because I'm *sure* it bothers him. Oh, and while we're on the subject of products of his subconscious, he sat at his drawing board this morning for an hour without drawing a line. Not one."

"Really?" This definitely made Paul's son think. He had flourished on the path his father had not pursued professionally. He had found a niche in sculpting his "concrete poems".

A rap music producer, who Joan had never even heard of, someone named Jet Black, had commissioned one, which Jeff had welded together out of titanium. It looked just like this:

b(all)s

except it was eight feet tall, twenty-four inches from front to back and sat on a titanium plate, which was an inch thick. Jet Black had enthusiastically paid $80,000 for it and proudly displayed it in the inner courtyard of his Hollywood Hills mansion. Ever since, *everyone* wanted a Jeff Warren. Jeff was now working on something he called "A Course In Miracles", which Oprah had her eye on. "Did he say anything about that?"

"Well, now we've come full circle. First, he asked if I'd like to fly out to see you kids for a few days, so we'll be coming into Albuquerque tomorrow night on the 10 or 10:30, more likely…"

"Terrific! I'll pick you up in this new hybrid I have. You won't believe it!" Jeff loved it when his parents came to Sante Fe. Before he was born, they had bought the little pueblo style house in the community known for its ability to attract artists to itself like a magnet attracts iron filings, in lieu of Paul's fleeing to Venice. Growing up, Jeff had looked forward to every trip there, until finally, after attending college at the University of New Mexico at Sante Fe, it had, de facto, become his home. Now he lived there with his wife, Alvina and their two-year-old son, Kurt, but since Paul's retirement, Joan and Paul would fly there several times a year and stay as long as they liked.

"Great, I'll let you know, when I'm sure of which flight. So… the second thing he asks is, and Jeff, I sure didn't have any answer for him, but I asked him why he hadn't drawn anything and he just looked at the empty paper and then at me and then he said, 'what if one of these people had a super-ego that was functioning perfectly well?' "

"Wow."

"Yeah. Wow. There's an answer. What did you expect? I'm no artist!"

Jeff loved his mother's sense of humor.

19.

The Bear

Ever since the black bear had first made his presence known in the summer of 2005, Albert Gustav had warned his sons repeatedly about the danger. He wasn't a "gun nut", but he made sure his two boys, Jack, who was twelve, and Billy, fourteen, knew how to shoot and were so well schooled in gun safety that it was automatic to them. Since it was clear that the bear was frequenting their property and the surrounding area, one couldn't be too careful and if they were even going into the yard, they had to keep the big creature in mind. Bears didn't want to confront a person any more than a person wanted to confront a bear, but should you suddenly come upon one another, you couldn't depend on the bear's reaction to be less than hostile. If the boys were to venture into the woods, they were to go armed. Armed for bear.

It was under these conditions that they sat on the east rail of the footbridge, with their fishing lines dangling in the Pendexter Brook and two Mossberg 12-gauge, pump-action, shotguns standing nearby, as the last of the July sun shown through the trees.

Dennie Bordeaux had left his truck behind on the trail shortly after turning off the road. He'd had to. Two large boulders had been strategically placed at either side of the path making it impossible for anything more than four and a half feet wide to pass between them. He'd jumped out and run to just south of this point in the brook, where it doglegged east for fifteen or twenty yards and the latest of many footbridges had been erected. He saw them through the trees facing his way, but was pretty sure that he'd ducked back behind a tree before they saw him. Two boys fishing, early teens. He stretched, craned his neck to peer over the brush. Shotguns. Two of 'em. Okay, now think. They're kids. You can tell 'em anything.

Stephanie felt she had been making tremendous progress due to the unexpected current of this little river, but she was still very wary of the east bank and every time the brook bent to the east, she felt it was turning toward him and it was all she could do to keep herself from climbing out onto the other shore and heading southwest on foot, but thus far she'd seen no break in the thick bramble on that side and she was quite relieved when the course of the brook would again turn more to the south. Now, as she was beginning to feel a little cold in the waning light, she seemed to be coming to yet another easterly bend in the stream, but on the western bank was a break in the vegetation! She swam for it. She was on her hands and knees, half out of the water, ready to run without catching her breath, when she sensed more than saw an enormous dark beast on the path before her, no more than six feet away. This was totally unfair! She couldn't believe she had run and swam and gotten away from that dirty scumrat and now she was going to be eaten by a bear!

Dennie stepped out onto the trail. Just say: having any luck, gentlemen? and get that first gun, he told himself. If only he had brought the stolen Kimber automatic, but who could have anticipated the need? He took a second step. A big dog barked. He froze.

"Murf!" shouted the younger boy, closest to the south bank.

"Murfy!" echoed the other, spinning around on the railing and hopping down to the deck of the bridge. "Come 'ere, boy!"

Dennie saw him lean his fishing pole on the rail and heft his Mossberg. Dennie stepped back behind the tree. He looked down at the blowgun in his left hand and felt seriously impotent.

Neither of the Gustav boys had ever seen a naked girl live and in person, so when their big, black Newfoundland emerged from the side path where they were looking and a petite teenaged blonde, without a stitch on, was hugging him about the neck, they were incredulous. Billy, the elder boy, stood blinking with his mouth agape. Jack's reaction was not dissimilar.

In a crisis, many people experience the sensation of time slowing down. Many more report that all of their senses are heightened (Stephanie would later say that, in the following moments, she could smell that it would soon rain). As Stephanie approached the bridge, she gained just enough elevation to pick out Dennie Bordeaux's face in the dense brush, maybe twenty yards away. She didn't hesitate for a heartbeat, but released the dog, took two steps on the bridge and snatched the Mossberg from a powerless Billy Gustav. She boldly strode to the north end of the bridge, leveling the gun on Bordeaux, as he pivoted to run, and squeezed the trigger, as Jack shouted, "Hey!"

But the trigger wouldn't squeeze and she realized the safety was on. She looked for it, saw the red button, pushed it off and raised the weapon again, but he was gone. She darted after him.

Jack looked at Billy, who was watching Stephanie disappear down the trail, his jaw still slack. Jack turned, jumped from the railing, grabbed his shotgun and ran after her, his older brother coming to his senses at this and joining along behind.

Dennie Bordeaux heard the pellets plinking off his right, front fender followed by the booming report of the shotgun, just as he arced onto the dirt road in a rapid reverse. He slammed the stick into first gear, spun all four wheels and tore off down the bumpy road, as Stephanie's second shot fell short.

Oh, Christ! This is it! Now I've got to run! thought Bordeaux. Alright, calm down. Just get home and get the guns, the emergency flight bag and the heads, shoot the fat shit, get back in the truck and go. You've planned for this. Not really even much to think about. They don't know who you are and it will take 'em a while to figure it out. This isn't good, but you've got enough of a head-start and you'll outsmart them yet! Just get home. Okay. Thirty minutes. Calm down.

At the first clap of thunder, Billy, who was just catching up to his brother and Stephanie, jumped and would ever after say that his first thought was that it was another gunshot.

Murf had reluctantly come to accept gunfire years earlier, but made a beeline for home at the sound of thunder. Jack simply watched him go, then calmly took his brother's gun from Stephanie, handed both of the Mossbergs to Billy and, turning back only halfway towards her, said, "Here, take my shirt." He quickly unbuttoned the red and black plaid cotton shirt and handed it to her, as the sky opened up.

"He kidnapped me!" she cried at them, as she buttoned up Jack's shirt, which was almost immediately drenched by the sudden summer cloudburst. "He kidnapped me and he was going to kill me!"

"We live near here," responded Jack. "You can call the Sheriff.

My mom and dad are there." He looked at his brother. "We can come back for the fishing gear, huh?"

20.

The Net

I t had been Paul's habit for many years to check his email accounts immediately after rising in the morning and he had used the mainpages of major news outlets as his homepage on each of the servers he favored. In the morning, after visiting the bathroom, he clicked on the Firefox icon that he kept in the middle of the dock hidden at the bottom of the screen on his iBook and the CBS News page came up. In a column in the center of the screen was a list of stories from around the nation. The top one read: Maine Serial Killer Stand-off Ends With Suicide. He clicked on it and began to read the details. Then he retrieved his cell phone from the bedside table and called Harvey Turner.

"The net was closing. We'd've been at his place by this morning anyhow, Paulo. We had his truck on the list of possibles from the immediate area. It's a miracle he even got home, but it rained like hell here from around sundown, right after he lost the girl and took off, 'til almost sun-up. People were taking shelter and we figure he took a back route, didn't get noticed or hit a roadblock. Anyway, we had his driver's license picture for owners of vehicle possibles and this girl IDed him right away. You'd love this kid, Paul. One tough cookie. He was lucky to get away from *her*!"

Harvey filled him in on the whole picture. He told him how the Bordeaux property had been surrounded just before midnight and Genevieve Bordeaux had picked up the phone on the second ring. She told them her son had pulled his truck into the garage out back hours earlier and not come out again, but he practically lived in there, so it wasn't alarming to her. She agreed to come to the door and they got her out of there and soon cleared the house. His mother said he didn't have a cell phone. He hated them. So the negotiator got on the speaker of a car at the end of the driveway and broadcast the first of many messages to Dennie Bordeaux and the hours in the Maine rain began.

Paul got the address of the Bordeaux home and had it up on Google Earth in a minute. He rotated it and noted its isolation by the surrounding pine woods and the adjacent Saco River. He zoomed out, got an idea of the surroundings and zoomed in on the two-car garage and rotated it.

Harvey told him how they'd waited out the rain, while they got no response from Dennie Bordeaux. When the rain had stopped and the sun was rising, the attack team had hooked cables to the garage doors, slipped the lock on the pedestrian door, fired in tear gas and a shock grenade, pulled the garage doors off their frames and gone in. Bordeaux was dead. He'd eaten a bullet from a Kimber .45. The gun had a homemade silencer. They didn't know when he'd done it, but he was cold.

Then Harvey told Paul what the reporters hadn't been told. He told him about the shrunken heads.

21.

Vanished Cultures

Saturday night in Sante Fe, Jeff and Alvina Warren hosted a little dinner party for a few friends and Jeff's parents. The guests included Andy Everly, the comedian, and his wife, Loretta, who had a jewelry business, Barry Fine, Andy's agent, and his girlfriend, Justine King, who had a lot of jewelry, the foursome in town for a long weekend, and local painter Ben DeSeni and his wife Cheeto, an author, who, between the two of them, had enough looks, brains, talent and personality to be a party in itself. Paul's curiosity had been aroused by a violin case that Cheeto had been good-naturedly protective of since her arrival. He wondered where it was right then.

He was beginning to get the idea that Andy had difficulty turning it off, once he had an audience. Excepting Paul, who had driven alone to Santa Rosa and back, they had all spent the day visiting Bonito, the Native American ceremonial city ruins in Chaco Canyon. Andy had been keeping everyone laughing, no matter what topic was raised, since the first course was served. He was in the middle of explaining how people in Alcoholics Anonymous were in denial about coffee and cigarettes being "mind altering" drugs.

"Please!!!" Please was his signature. "I'm a different person, before I've had my coffee in the morning!" he waited for the laughter. "It's the absence of the drug and the withdrawal symptoms that can be alleviated by it, that demonstrate that it's mind altering...

Why do you think it's called a nicotine fit?… You're jonesin' and a smoke makes your mind 'normal' again!"

There was agreeable laughter all around, though nobody was smoking and, in fact, none of them did smoke anymore, not even Andy.

"But I've got a theory related to what we saw today." The conversation had earlier turned to the native cultures that had vanished from the New Mexico and Arizona area, some leaving behind pueblos that looked as if the people had simply walked away en masse, others, like the cliff dwellers, leaving evidence of having withdrawn into an apparent siege situation. Currently, evidence of cannibalism at some of the latter was a topic of controversy. Paul had offered his theory about it earlier and now the comedian was riffing on that. "I think it's clear that the thing all great ancient societies share is that they rose to greatness after first becoming obsessed with and then suppressing football…

"Think about it. Every time an archaeological dig unearths some great ancient temple or city, they're insistent about stressing how many football fields it covers! Please!! This can't be a coincidence!"

Jeff laughed. He nudged his dad. "He's such a wing-nut."

"He's clever. A little twisted. I liked the bit about the presidency of Russia, though it's kind of dated, doesn't really apply to Putin, of course," said Paul.

"Yeah, but it still works, because we all remember Yeltzin. He likes to tell people that he almost sold that joke to Letterman." Dinner was over. Jeff stood, picked up his coffee, indicated to his dad that he do the same. "Come on," he said.

They were dining on the stone patio, under a star filled sky, behind the house. Jeff led Paul over to the cactus garden, sipped his coffee and looked him in the eye; trying to sound non-chalant, but feeling conspiratorial, he asked, "So what's the scoop with Santa Rosa, Dad?"

Paul didn't hesitate. He looked at his son and matter-of-factly answered, "Keep this to yourself, please, Jeff. Somebody's killing serial killers. I don't know who, but I'm sure the pattern's there."

Jeff was speechless. Paul continued, "Whoever he is, he's finding people now that are still UNSUBS to the Bureau and, worst of all, they don't know he's doing it."

22.

Probability

Paul told his son about Arlen Wesley Henniford and how there was nothing he had observed about the scene of his death to indicate that it hadn't been staged.

He said that the massive overdose of cocaine that had killed Kevin Pimental seemed fishy, not only because Pimental was apparently destitute, but especially in light of the fact that he may have been in the company of an unknown stranger. The last known sighting of him had been on a liquor store surveillance camera, which captured him walking away with an unidentifiable person, who may or may not have been waiting for him.

Harvey Turner had been certain that Dennie Bordeaux's death was a suicide, but his mentioning that the team who stormed the garage had "slipped" the lock on the pedestrian door had raised Paul's suspicions and he had asked Harvey to fax him all the photos of the Bordeaux scene. Sure enough, it was equipped with a spring bolt that could easily have been jimmied with anything like a credit card or strip of flexible metal. Had an adversary been lying in wait, the Bordeaux scene may also easily have been staged.

Lastly, Jerome Anthony's hanging in Santa Rosa appeared to fit the pattern. He had stepped off of his basement stairs, with a noose around his neck. Paul had seen it before, but it was very unusual. In fact he'd seen it used to stage fake suicides before and, in his estimation, he was seeing that again. He only wished he could have visited the basement when it was still a fresh scene. That afternoon he'd had to settle for photos, a house that had been completely remodeled and an interview with Anthony's former employer, who was cooperative, but clearly preoccupied with his business and who made no secret of the fact that he'd been traumatized by the event and wasn't awfully happy about having to revisit it in his memory.

"Surely you told Harvey what you think," Jeff insisted.

"Before I went up to Ogdensburg, I told him I was working on a theory, but no, I haven't told him what it is. Frankly, I'm wishing I hadn't told you."

"Does Mom know?"

Paul looked across the small yard to Joan, still seated at the table with Kurt, her two-year-old grandson, in her lap, conversing with her daughter-in-law. She glanced up at him. "I haven't told her, Jeff, but your mother is the smartest woman I know. There's no telling what she knows."

"Yeah, tell me about it. Between the two of you, I never got away with anything."

"You were a good kid, Jeff." Paul looked his son in the eye with a father's deep love and remembered how close they had come to losing him. A drunk driver had struck him while he was riding his bike one summer afternoon, when he was ten, and he had lain in a coma for six days, horribly broken. "We never had any behavioral problems with you, to speak of."

Jeff was about to reply, but Paul could see him looking beyond his right shoulder and turned to see Andy Everly closely approaching.

"Paul," Andy implored, "Settle an argument for me, would you? Was Albert DeSalvo really the Boston Strangler? I got in a discussion with a friend before going on one night at The Comedy Store and it got so heated that when I went on, my focus was all off and I bombed something awful! So what's your professional opinion?"

Through the French doors to the dining room, Paul could see that Cheeto had taken her violin and bow from their case and, as she emerged from the house checking her tuning, it seemed they were about to be entertained. She came to the freestanding fireplace at the north end of the patio, stopped and turned to face the table and began to play. Paul immediately recognized the Gershwin brothers' "Fascinatin' Rhythm", an old favorite of his. He smiled.

Then he looked again at Andy, who stood awaiting a reply, and said, "Short answer: DeSalvo was a burglar, with an overactive libido and some odd fetishes, but in all probability, he wasn't the strangler. Excuse me."

Then he took his coffee and strode back to his seat.

23.

Virtuosos

Cheeto's rendition of "Fascinatin' Rhythm" was truly fascinating to Paul. She played it just like the great Stephane Grappelli. Paul was intimately familiar with Grappelli's music and was delighted when she followed it with another of his standards, "Taking A Chance On Love", yet by the time she'd finished this tune, he was dumbfounded by something else. He suddenly realized that she bore a startling resemblance to the way Joan had looked when they met. Joan had worked as an interpreter for the State Department. She had been a blonde then, though her natural color was a deep reddish brown. How could he have not noticed this right away?

"You think she looks like me when I was interpreting at State, I'll bet," came his wife's voice in his ear.

"I suddenly feel like I'm being set up," he looked at her, standing at his right shoulder, inches away and said, "but I just noticed the similarity."

"I know. I watched your face change. You looked like you'd suddenly seen a ghost!"

"Well, *she* pales by comparison, Joanie! What can I say?" he laughed.

"Good save, Sherlock. What would you say to a little stargazin' later?" As long as they had owned the house, they had appreciated the beauty of its pueblo style architecture, including that two flat areas of the roof could be utilized as living or sleeping space.

Stargazing had been their codeword for making love under the open night sky.

"You're the most brilliant star I know and I could gaze at you all night." Paul murmured.

"Wow! You're looking for something special. What the hell are you drinking, anyhow?" Joan kidded him.

"Coffee and I've *got* something special." He kissed her, glanced at Cheeto, who was now playing something that he didn't recognize and said, "You know, I think I didn't see it, because I've always preferred the red. I don't think of you as a blonde."

"You'd better not think of any blondes, buster!" She poked him in the ribs, then giving him a squeeze whispered, "Or no sixty-eight!"

He feigned shock. Then he asked Joan, who was the best lip-reader he'd ever known, if she happened to pick up what Cheeto had said before she began playing what she now was.

"She said it's called Tears of Joy," answered Joan.

When Cheeto had finished playing and had received grateful applause, she put her instrument away in the house, then joined them all on the patio.

"Paul is a big fan of Stephane Grappelli, Cheeto. You couldn't have made him happier tonight," Joan complimented the younger woman and pinched her husband, knowing that he would appreciate the truth in the double entendre.

He resisted reacting, of course. He said, "Who would have guessed you're an author and not a professional musician?"

"I'm very good at imitation," Cheeto admitted, "but I have no style of my own. What's more, I play for pleasure. I'm sure I'd find the business of pursuing a living at it joyless. I'm a homebody, you see; a real nester, so writing has been ideal for me."

"And joyful?" asked Paul.

"And joyful," she affirmed. "I enjoy every aspect of it. I research and write about what interests me most. I have a great agent and I don't do book tours."

"Oh?" said Joan.

"The trick is to not be *too* successful," she laughed. "I write about virtuosos. Biographies. The people who are going to buy my book about Itzhak Perlman will buy it, whether I do a tour or not, so I stay here."

"Sounds like you found just the right niche," said Joan.

"I'm quite sure I did. There is no place like New Mexico!" Cheeto exclaimed. Then she said to Paul, "I understand you had something similar in mind, when you bought this place."

"What's that?" he asked.

"Staying put and being an artist."

"Oh. No. Actually, we bought this place instead of my going to Italy to stay put and be an artist," corrected Paul. "And like you with the violin, I think the pursuit of a living as an artist wouldn't have been the right choice of lifestyles."

He knew, also, that he had been a virtuoso in his chosen field.

24.

Orion

Paul was sitting at his drawing board sketching with pen and ink, when he heard Joan's voice say, "I thought you'd be painting." He looked up to see that she appeared just as he would have expected her to, except that her hair was blond. He realized he was dreaming. "I'm drawing a virtuoso," he found himself replying, as he looked at his work, which had not yet become a discernible landscape.

"Was Albert DeSalvo really the Boston Strangler?" he heard Cheeto ask and, turning to look at his wife, found Cheeto standing there examining the drawing.

He looked at the drawing board again and found it had become a map of the U.S. and Canada, with brightly colored push-pins indicating the locations of crime scenes, like they'd used before the age of the computer to figure out a subject's area of operation and try to determine where he was based.

He opened his eyes and the sky over Sante Fe looked like a dark map covered in white push-pins. To the lower left in this expanse, the constellation Orion stood out. As he focused on the three stars of its belt, he thought he could make out a grid and, glancing around now, he could see that it clearly seemed to be there, superimposed on the entire sky. He realized he was still dreaming, squeezed his eyes tightly and when he opened them, he was lying beside Joan beneath a morning sky into which the sun was just beginning to inch.

25.

Ritual

Paul did some of his best thinking while driving. It was the effect of having to concentrate on a continuous task that was simple enough that it left his mind free to wander. Things would suddenly come to him behind the wheel of a car that he would never have thought of had he been sifting through files or deep in a brainstorming session. It held true with conversations he would have when driving, as well. Joan had always loved listening to him talk while he was driving. He relaxed.

His greatest breakthroughs, however, often occurred during his morning shower. Paul took it for granted that the robotic morning ritual, combined with not yet having been distracted by the day's onslaught of stimuli, plus the residual reshuffling of the night's dreams, were collectively responsible for how often he would suddenly see a complete picture where there had only been puzzle pieces, during the act of shampooing his hair.

This morning Paul was already thinking about the fact that he didn't know what bothered him most about his virtuoso hunter. This guy was truly unique. He was highly organized, highly resourceful, his area of operation was enormous, he was finding serial killers that the FBI had been unable to catch and in the case of the Santa Rosa murders, nobody had even realized a serial murderer was active in the area, he was using a different method of killing every time and always made the death appear to be accidental or suicide.

With the exception of Pimental, the killers had been found with at least some of the remains of their victims and cases had been closed.

This is all about motive, Paul was thinking over and over, like a mantra.

He was glad that Jeff hadn't asked him why he hadn't told Harvey what he believed yet. He was trying to imagine how this could not be someone, or worse yet, more than one someone, in law enforcement. It was this that he was thinking about, while picturing the scene in Jerome Anthony's basement and washing his right foot, when it dawned on him that the Anthony murder could not have been this UNSUB's first and if he'd seen the death scene while it was fresh, he knew he'd have realized this immediately.

26.

Message

Ordinarily what would be most outstanding about Orion (by the time Paul had put his socks on, he had decided to codename his UNSUB Orion) was the fact that the last two killings were only days apart. Normally this escalation would indicate that the killer was spinning out of control, but this was usually accompanied by a breakdown in organization and often led directly to the killer's apprehension. Paul didn't think Orion was spinning out of control. If anything, he was becoming more refined. Paul didn't see any indication of disorganization and he intuited that Orion had killed Henniford at his earliest convenience once he had either figured out who he was or, more likely, once he had discovered his dump site and he probably had followed with Bordeaux so soon afterward simply because he had only just figured out who he was or, again more likely, determined where he lived, and again it was convenient.

Paul knew there was something else, too. Orion was sending a message. These last two killings, especially that of Bordeaux, had been right under their noses. Of course, he may have been trying to send a message all along. With the exception of Pimental, whose victims had been left in public places, Orion had been careful to have them all found with their victims. He was telling them he was doing this because of what these men had done. At the same time, he was smart enough not to make it obvious that the murders were murders, so with any luck they wouldn't be pursuing him. No doubt, he looked at this whole enterprise like he was doing them, and society as a whole, a favor.

Whoever Orion was, he had to have the funds that allowed him to bear the expense of the travel involved, but he also had to be free to do so and presumably in such a way that he could not be easily connected to being in the area of his killings when they occurred. Business might be a cover, but it generally left an accurate record and required interaction with others. It's difficult to establish an alibi on a business trip, if you need time to slip away to kill. Paul was beginning to imagine someone on vacation. No. On safari.

27.

Behavioral Norms

The Sunday morning blueberry pancake breakfast was a Warren family tradition going back to at least the time of Paul's childhood and now Jeff's family rarely saw a Sunday without stacks of buttermilk flapjacks filled with juicy blueberries, butter, maple syrup, eggs, bacon, toast, jellies, fruit juices, coffee, milk and fresh sliced fruit (Paul preferred peaches) and vanilla ice cream for desert.

Andy, Loretta, Barry and Justine had spent the night in a motel, but joined them for breakfast, before heading off to Las Vegas for a week long gig. Paul was mainly enjoying the fare and the company of his grandson, but the conversation had largely been directed by Andy, who seemed comparatively serious this morning, to the differences between abnormal and criminal psychology. Paul had explained, in sort of an off hand way, that criminal psychology was a sub-category of abnormal psychology, that psychology was a behavioral science and that people's psychological make-up could actually only be *implied* by observing their behavior. This would, of course, include what they reported about themselves. Criminal behavior implied a criminal psychology.

"In rehabilitation efforts these days, the talk is all about 'norms'," Paul told Andy, "not laws or rules, but norms, because they're trying to emphasize that you'll never fit in, if your behavior doesn't conform to the behavioral norms of your society, whatever your psychological make-up."

"What I want to know is…" Andy was apparently warming up now, "was Einstein normal?"

"Einstein was abnormal!" insisted Jeff. "He was an anomaly, even among his peers."

"Lousy violinist, too," said Barry.

Paul said, "But what matters is that however abnormal his psyche was, his behavior wasn't criminal…"

"You never heard him play the violin!" Andy shot back.

"…or dangerous," concluded Paul.

"Not counting encouraging the development of the atom bomb, of course," said Alvina, who, like many of *her* peers, was outspokenly anti-nuclear.

"And while I wouldn't argue that that wasn't dangerous, it wasn't criminal," said Paul and, turning to Andy, attempted to sum up, "and ultimately, I'm concerned with criminal behavior, which isn't normal."

"What about what this guy Bordeaux said?" asked Barry. "That sign they say he had on his bedroom wall that said 'among headhunters, the one that won't kill people is dysfunctional'? Don't think I'm being facetious, but wouldn't he have been right about the norms of *that* society?"

"The point that he was missing is that he didn't live in a society of headhunters," answered Paul.

Andy asked, "You don't think he was trying to make the point that we *are* a society of headhunters?"

"We're only a society of headhunters," answered Paul, "if we allow his kind to dominate our society."

28.

"The Redheads"

When Paul was almost five years old, his parents bought a home in Hamilton, Ohio and moved the family from the first floor of the two family house they had shared with Paul's paternal grandmother in Cincinnati and their lives all began a new phase. Paul's new neighborhood was more suburban in character. There was less traffic and the houses were primarily for single families. There was a grammar school just around the corner. Behind it was an enormous playground, with swings and ballfields and a large covered sandbox. Though he was too young to understand the effects of this at the time, his neighbors were, by and large, on a higher income level than those in Cincinnati.

Paul was looking forward to meeting all the new kids in the neighborhood and at school in the fall. He was sorry to have left behind an awful lot of friends in Cincinnati for a four-year-old and needed to be consoled with the assurance that he'd see them in the years to come during visits to and stays at his grandmother's place. He was not sorry, was in fact relieved, to have left behind a family who lived a hundred yards away from his old house, people they had known simply as "the redheads." They were a large brood of tough Irish kids who aggressively defended the block where they lived and bullied all who approached. For the rest of his life, Paul would be aware of the fact that, though they would never really know him nor he them, "the redheads" had set in place a dynamic that would shape his life, because he was already regularly pondering the question of why, if he hadn't done anything wrong to anyone, he should have to defend his right to be on a public street.

In time Paul would learn that the natural system of organization in human society was the dominance hierarchy, with an "Alpha" individual at the top of a pyramid of layers of individuals of lesser and lesser status. It was a system maintained by aggression, actual or threatened, and it could be seen throughout the animal kingdom, as well. He would also become familiar with the theory that in every relationship, one person is more dominant and one more submissive and he would, for the most part, come to accept it as true, but like most American kids, he knew he had rights and that he lived in a society with laws that everyone was supposed to obey.

Paul's father was an electrical engineer and an ex-marine who had fought on Okinawa and Guam during the second world war. His mom had been a legal secretary. They were intelligent and well educated and wanted at least as much for their kids. They worked hard to provide it. In later years Paul would wonder just how much aggression the war had taken out of his father. Jim Warren never talked about the war. He was a quiet man with few close friends, who did crossword and letter substitution puzzles, watched this new television thing like he'd pioneered the idea himself and ate and drank too much. Paul was always amazed at the pictures of his dad he'd look at in his grandmother's photo album, because his father had been so thin. All of Paul's life, Jim Warren had been overweight.

Paul's father taught him how to draw, how to build a radio and how to build a house. He taught him songs to sing, how to build a fire to cook hot dogs and hamburgers and how to ride a bike. Later he'd show him how to maintain and repair it and Paul, who already loved to take things apart and put them back together, took to it like a duck to water and he would enjoy a reputation that would last throughout his college years of piloting bikes and cars he had thrown together that others would literally be afraid of. Paul's father would repeatedly tell him, "They won't pay you for who you are; they'll pay you for what you know." He taught him to play baseball and tutored him at math. He taught him how to solve letter substitution puzzles, but he didn't teach him to fight. Oh, maybe a few moves at times when Paul would have trouble with a bully in junior high, but it hadn't been in the curriculum while he was being raised.

One night, several summers after they had moved to Hamilton, the Warrens went to a drive-in movie and during the second feature, while Paul was dozing off, he heard an actor in the film say, "It's the law of the jungle: kill or be killed," and he immediately related this to "the redheads." He had already come to a conclusion about people from having noted that there were kids in Hamilton who behaved similarly to "the redheads". He had divided kids into good kids and tough kids. Good kids seemed to be smarter and they didn't get in a lot of trouble. Tough kids were like little criminals and tried to dominate the good kids and each other. He wondered about the difference between these kids long and hard, on the Sunday afternoon that followed having been to the drive-in. He concluded that the difference between the two sets of kids was their parents, that good kids' parents cared enough to teach them to be good and tough kids' parents apparently didn't care about their being good and probably taught them the law of the jungle. Being a good kid, he decided the tough kids' parents were wrong.

29.

Motive

At the root of the dominance hierarchy lies competition: competition for the choice of whatever is desirable, be it territory, sustenance, possessions, or sexual partners. It has been argued that sexual aggression is at the root of all competition.

Paul had always had an attitude about competition and even he wasn't exactly certain why it was what it was. His older sister, Jenny, had been the most competitive and, arguably, the best athlete in the family, excelling at team sports. Paul, on the other hand, while an exceptional center-fielder, preferred individual sports and had shone at running cross-country and track and field events, particularly distance running.

Paul had become more and more selective about games until he got to the point where he claimed not to play any, though in truth he could be depended on to accept an invitation to play softball or touch football because he loved them and didn't take them seriously and he would also play volleyball or badminton, but only if the strict rules of the sport were observed. But Paul hadn't played a game of cards since his twenties and you couldn't pay him to play ping-pong. He'd played chess since his dad taught him as a child, but it no longer interested him.

Of course, he admitted to himself that he competed in his own way by being good at what he chose to do. He'd always had the type of self-confidence that said the kind of people he respected would recognize what he had to offer. He had outright refused to compete for women for the same reason and he knew, when he thought of Joan, that he had been right.

The overall scheme of things was about competition, though, and there was no getting around it. It was why he was who he was. Paul believed that man had come out of nature to rise above the law of the jungle. It was probably the influence of his Jesuit educators that caused him to think humanity had made this move to use the power of numbers to defend the weak against the dominant. Paul had committed to using his mind to stop bullies from attempting to act like alpha individuals.

The motives and behaviors of a serial killer are not to be confused with what we call "normal sexual aggression." The mis-shaped psyche of the serial murderer is sexually stimulated by the acts of violence he performs and very often the terror he instills in those he is in control of. Control, domination, is always a key component in why he does what he does. He is always attempting to conquer his feelings of *not* having control and he is doomed to failure. After a cooling off period, he is forced to kill again.

Paul knew, however, that this did not apply to Orion and the reason was simple. Orion wasn't sexually motivated. He was stim-seeking, though he'd probably deny it, but that wasn't his primary motive either. Orion was motivated by revenge.

30.

Long Division

When Paul and Joan purchased the house in Sante Fe, the first thing Paul did was convert the second bedroom to a studio. After Jeff's arrival, it soon returned to being a bedroom and Paul added a large lean-to structure to the side of the garage, mainly of glass construction. Jeff still used this space for smaller projects, but with his large sculptures, he had needed a much larger work area and for years he had been leasing a small warehouse. It was there that he was completing work on his newest concrete poem sculpture, *A Course In Miracles*. Paul was seeing it for the first time on Sunday afternoon, as Jeff was finalizing the burnishing and polishing phase of the massive titanium piece.

Jeff explained to his father that *A Course In Miracles* was a 1600 page tome, said to be "channeled" from Christ to the mind of its authoress, over a period of seven or eight years. Essentially, it makes the claim that all misunderstanding arises from the misguided idea that one can be separate from God and that salvation comes in the acceptance of the reality that one is "at one with" God.

Jeff's sculpture was a nine and a half foot tall example of an equation in long division, just like one would see in a grammar school textbook, with the long division sign separating three identical versions of the word "one." One divided by one is one.

"The idea is that we are all 'one in Christ' and Christ is at one with God The Father, The Creator of all that is real," said Jeff. "Not really different from traditional Christianity. But what 'The Course'

stresses is that, because one has had the thought that one is separate from God, an entire space-time continuum of illusion, based
on division, has appeared in one's 'Godly' mind and it has been
accepted as reality, because it has been so well imagined. Things
immediately become complicated by separating the self into bil-
lions of egos all over the place throughout time and the text insists
that the ego's only purpose is to convince one that the illusion is
real. So the method of correction is to 'forgive' the illusion and
accept that one actually exists in the 'eternal now', at one with one's
Creator, because there simply is no satisfactory alternative available
in this ungodly universe. This, of course, would be in keeping with
Christ's statement: 'My kingdom is not of this world' and, at the
same time, seems to me to be consistent with Buddhist thinking."

"I can see why you boiled it down to this," said Paul.

"Most answers can be expressed in very simple terms, once you
know the answer to begin with. 'The Course' says acceptance of
'the at-one-ment' is *the* answer. I simply restated the problem and
the solution in a mathematical equation that we can all accept as a
simple truth."

"Good job."

31.

Above The Clouds

"*A Course In Miracles* likes to stress things like the idea that everyone seeks happiness and fails to find it, until they seek it at its source, the self that is with its Creator, and once one has this joyful awareness, it's just a matter of remembering to remember it," Jeff told his father, "To remember to let go of the perception that you are separate from God and embrace the knowledge that you are not."

Paul didn't like to talk about it, but beginning in high school, he had been what he would have said was a "lapsed Catholic." Throughout his years at Notre Dame, there had, of course, been church attendance, but it had become less frequent until it virtually ceased after his graduation. Jeff's reference to "this ungodly universe" had surprised him only in who was using the adjective.

"So what we're doing here is shifting responsibility for the state of the world from God to man, at the same time that we're saying 'it isn't real, so don't worry, be happy'," observed Paul.

"That's pretty close," agreed Jeff. " 'The Course' says, 'you are the dreamer of the dream'. I like to think of it this way: the universe is our ultimate practical joke on ourselves; eventually, everyone goes to Heaven, because no one ever left Heaven."

Paul was replaying this conversation in his mind, as he dozed off in his seat aboard a DC10 over Elkhart, Kansas, on Wednesday afternoon.

32.

What Happened In Vegas

Paul was standing in the hallway of the courthouse in Las Vegas, Nevada with Harvey Turner and Mrs. Thomas McAdams, Shirley, the mother of a murdered girl. Now there was a commotion in the mass of people behind him in the hall, reporters mostly. Apparently the paperwork had been completed and Andrew Travis Johansen was about to join them in the hallway. Paul was suddenly terrified and he knew he knew why and knew just as clearly that he wouldn't be able to do anything about the reason why, because somehow whatever it was had already happened. He began to turn toward the commotion and he caught Harvey's eyes widening as he looked past Paul at whatever it was. This scared him even more and he tried to turn faster, but felt like he was moving under water against the force of the stifling humidity and his inner awareness of the futility of trying.

As he completed his turn, out of the fifty or sixty people in that part of the hall, reporters extending microphones and beginning to shout questions, lights and TV cameras, and although the man was among those farthest away from him, Paul immediately focused on Tom McAdams. Tom's attention, like that of everyone around him, seemed to be riveted on Andrew Travis Johansen, and as he closed the distance between himself and his daughter's murderer, who was now only steps away from the intersection of the north corridor of the T-shaped hallway where Paul, Harvey, Shirley McAdams and the Smithsons were, Paul was sure, from the look on his face, Tom needed to be stopped. Paul started to shout, knowing it wouldn't help and, as he remembered what happened next, he awoke with a start in his seat next to Joan on the DC10.

33.

Obsession

Ancient wisdom tells us that one can be said to be three things: what one is believed to be by others, what one believes oneself to be and what one truly is.

When searching for the identity of a serial killer, what others see him as is what keeps him from being identified, for as normal or as odd as he appears to be, he won't appear to be who he really is.

Who he believes himself to be may be more helpful, especially if he gives you clues to what he believes. Frequently, as in the cases of BTK, The Zodiac or The Black Dahlia Murderer, an UNSUB will actually communicate with authorities and often he will attempt to explain why he is doing what he does and this betrays who he believes himself to be.

Usually, this also indicates to an experienced profiler what is at the heart of the killer's obsession. Having a good idea of what any serial perpetrator is obsessed with is generally the greatest clue to learning who he really is.

34.

Experience and Control

Paul had a professor in college, Dr. Harry Haak, who he considered to be one of the best educators he had ever met. Dr. Haak had said, "People learn from *whatever* happens, so good teaching involves controlling what happens."

Paul was thinking about that Friday morning, as he sat at his computer reviewing data on unsolved serial murders and multiple similar missing persons cases across the country, looking for evidence of a killer who had been stopped, but whom they had not become aware of, someone preceding Jerome Anthony Anthony.

Everyone is a product of their genes, their environment and their experience. Something in the experience of serial predators leads them all, whatever their obsession is, to have a common need to prove to themselves they are in control.

In Paul's experience, one could expect that after each act of violence, the sense of having control would wear off and eventually the cycle would repeat itself, because the underlying feelings of inadequacy that drive the need for control never really go away. So a predator will continue to prey until caught. In most cases there will be a visible evolution in his crimes toward what he imagines the fantasy to be that might most satisfy him. But unless he is indisposed for some reason, such as sickness, imprisonment, military service or death, he'll keep doing what he does over and over, until he is stopped.

There are very rare exceptions, like Edmund Kemper III, who

shot his grandparents to death at fourteen and after being freed as an adult, killed six young women in the Santa Cruz, California area, before he finally bludgeoned and decapitated his mother and killed her best friend. Apparently he felt he'd finally done what drove him to it all, because he then called the authorities and asked them to come and get him. Kemper has offered investigators tremendous insight into the phenomenon of the serial killer psyche, but he's not alone. Many serial predators have been surprisingly forthcoming, once they were imprisoned. It's a way for them to get attention and attempt to exercise control, a way to feel powerful and important. All the same, Bundy, Gacy, Dahmer, Kemper, BTK, most of them who would talk at all added to the authorities understanding before their time to go arrived. Bundy, in fact, had been shocked that he was actually going to be executed when he felt he had so much more he could teach them!

A series of five young girls had been abducted and found dead along a stretch of Rte. 88 between Schenectady and Schoharie, N.Y., in the year before Anthony's hanging. The abduction murders had stopped without a suspect being apprehended, but after speaking to the D.A. in Albany, Paul was convinced that a man in a mental hospital, who had confessed, was, in all likelihood, the killer.

Now he was focused on a group of disappearances of girls and young women from Juneau, Alaska in that same year. Nine females, ages seventeen to thirty had vanished suddenly without a word: a college student, a nurse, a waitress, a deckhand on a salmon trawler, two exotic dancers, a cashier in a grocery market, a bartender and a stay-at-home mother. To this day there was speculation that every one of them had left of her own volition. Only the seventeen-year-old college freshman was a native Alaskan and one of her friends thought she had seen going away to college as having provided her with the opportunity to flee the state altogether. Even the stay-at-home mom drew rumors of affairs and her husband's frantic protests did nothing to change that. However, the more authorities looked, the more they were convinced that each of these women had made no preparations to leave, each had told nobody where she was going, none left a trail or had ever been heard from again and all had apparently left everything behind except what they had been wearing and carrying. Three had left their identification behind. After almost exactly a year, there were no more unexplained disappearances. Suspects were questioned and released. There were a few debunked confessions. Nobody was ever arrested in the case and it all went cold.

Paul found the number for the D.A.'s office in Juneau, punched the digits on his phone and clicked back to the news article about the salmon boat deckhand, while he listened to the ringing.

35.

Games

Dr. Harry Haak had drawn the distinction between play, games and sport. While all three suspended the rules of everyday reality, to varying degrees they all took on rules of their own. Play was generally less regulated and carried on mainly for fun. Games were a more structured form of play and were regulated through a variety rules. They could be played for fun, but very often were played for more serious reasons. Sport was an even more structurally organized and regulated level of game playing. The reasons behind sport fill volumes.

Dr. Haak was essentially a professor of principals of education, but in truth he was a sociologist.

Paul was on a Monday morning flight to Alaska, thinking about territory and games. Paul had withdrawn from game playing more and more beginning in childhood. His problem was with cheaters, kids who wouldn't play by the rules, but insisted they hadn't broken them. It took all the fun out of the experience and then what was the point of playing? If you challenged them, things soon escalated into real world aggression and Paul was then doubly exasperated at the total unfairness of having to fight or back down, when the other person was wrong in every respect. Kids were always breaking the rules in games and getting away with it. He was truly grateful for the adult supervision and regulation that came with organized sports.

It seemed to Paul there was a parallel relationship between the ethics of all of this and those seen in the practice of man's territoriality and indeed many games were territorial in nature, the Japanese game of Go and American football being only two of the better examples. Territoriality played an enormous role in human psychology.

Paul was flying to Juneau to study the territory from which nine women had vanished. He was doing this to determine how Orion had found their abductor and he was sure that he had. If he was successful, he hoped to find remains of them and their abductor, because they were all long dead, of course.

He mainly was hoping to see something in the territory that would give him a better idea of just how Orion had discovered the Juneau abductor and he was becoming convinced that learning the territory and the habits of the killers had been the key to each of Orion's successes thus far, except perhaps Pimental, though he wasn't completely certain about it. In fact, the only things he was sure of were that Orion was only killing men who murdered young women and that he was having what he believed to be his righteous revenge.

He was making an educated guess that Orion had begun in Juneau and for some reason, perhaps related to his being a beginner, he had failed to leave the abductor's body where it would be quickly found.

36.

Joan

When Joan said she was no artist, she wasn't kidding, however her appreciation of the arts was unparalleled, especially those that involved language. Joan lived for passion and she was passionate about passion expressed artfully in words. She never so much as kept a personal journal, but she devoured the writing of others and she knew more song lyrics than Wolfman Jack.

What had impressed Paul, shortly after they had met, was witnessing the amount of English language poetry with which she was intimately familiar. Of course at that point, he was still thinking of her as a young Italian girl. He was almost fifteen years her senior. Joan was American by birth, however she had been raised in Italy. Her father had worked for the U.S. Diplomatic Corps (Paul had taken it for granted that he was a spy, but never learned for certain one way or the other) and had met her mother, shortly after his arrival in Rome, in 1961. Gina Spadafora spoke seven languages and was working as an interpreter for her government, at the time. No doubt, though she would become fluent in only five, Joan's love of language, and the things that could be done with it, stemmed from her mother.

Her love of art came from Italy itself, an unavoidable thing, if one's eyes and ears are open in a country so steeped in art that no other can quite compare to it.

Her charm came from her father. President John Fitzgerald Kennedy had once said, "I believe that Randall Cook is the most charming fellow I have ever had the pleasure to know." This was nothing to sneeze at. In his time, JFK had been acquainted with some snake charmers.

Joan stood at Paul's drawing table now, looking at the sketch that was, thus far, just a hundred or so random-seeming short lines. She'd come into the studio looking for the dog. Rufrak hadn't been quite himself since they'd picked him up at the Turners', when they returned from Santa Fe. Harvey and Janice's four kids always ran him ragged, but she was quite sure that was why, after he'd had a stay at the Turner place, they usually almost had to drag him to the car. He never wanted to leave. This time he had jumped in the Jeep as soon as Paul had opened his door to get out. Harvey had no explanation, nor did any of the Turners. Rufrak had been as normal as spring rain up until Joan's call, twenty minutes earlier, to say they were on their way from the airport to get him and then, when Harvey and Janice and all the kids had called him, he failed to come and couldn't be found. They'd been near panic, when Paul and Joan pulled in the driveway and the retriever had come bolting across their front lawn. Joan had been standing at the drawing table for a minute or so, when the dog barked behind her. She was startled and jumped at the sound of it.

"Rufrak!" she exclaimed, whirling around to see him cowering behind a cabinet in the corner. She took two steps in his direction, holding her hands out to him, asking, "What has gotten into you, puppy?"

"I think I know the answer to that," came Harvey Turner's voice from the doorway, startling Joan for the second time in thirteen seconds.

37.

Landings

From the air above Juneau, the city looks so small, one could be forgiven for thinking there's only an airport below; when one could see it at all, of course. Tonight it was raining in Juneau. The city was covered in clouds and they were all Paul could see from his widow, as his plane arced around in its approach to landing.

Paul was always a little worried during landings and take-offs. He knew that statistically they were the most likely times for accidents. The numbers showed that landing in bad weather was the most common situation in which crashes occurred. He also knew that some of the best pilots in the world flew in Alaska, but that the outstanding ones among them were the bush pilots, guys that took off from, and landed their small planes in, places you'd swear a helicopter would be hard pressed to park. He knew that flying was statistically safer than driving, but the truth was that the law of gravity and the flimsiness of aircraft and human bodies always scratched on Paul's medulla oblongata, from the time a landing began, until the plane was taxiing to a terminal. To make matters worse, tonight they were apparently landing in a thunderstorm. He swallowed once again and his ears popped.

38.

War Babies

What came to be known as "the baby boom" in America was the spike in births that came with the prosperity that followed the second world war and the return home of millions of young men eager to take the best life had to offer. The nineteen-fifties became a time of myth and legend that gave birth to rock and roll, the space age and nuclear standoff.

Paul remembered the fifties with a feeling of inexpressible nostalgia. It was the best of times, the peak of life in this country. He always thought of it as a time when the edge of town was visibly definable, not just the start of another town, a time when there were woods at the end of dead end streets and fields beyond the last house.

Orion simply believed that the creation of the atomic bomb marked the beginning of the decline of modern civilization. Orion was a person whose destiny would be almost entirely cast by the mind that grasped the fifties as a wonderful, but terrifying time. He was deeply fearful of the potential behind the "duck and cover" and shoulder to shoulder line-up in the hall drills he and his schoolmates were put through. It had been impressed upon him that there were millions of people starving "overseas" and as a young boy he had thought the smartest, safest and perhaps even kindest thing to do was to put them out of their misery before they came charging over here to take what we had. He never voiced this idea to anyone, but he wasn't alone in formulating it.

It's worthy of note that when JFK was president, his Chairman of the Joint Chiefs of Staff, Army General Lyman Lemnitzer, advocated a policy of nuclear war sooner than later, while we had the greatest advantage, because he was convinced that it was inevitable. He wasn't alone either, by any means. Far from it.

Orion learned to keep his ideas to himself when, after first learning about hypnotism, he suggested that you could hypnotize someone to steal or kill and you'd be safe, even if they were caught or killed. His father had admonished him that the plotter of a deed is as responsible for the deed as the doer, that a boy with his "gifts" should be ashamed at having such criminal ambitions and that a real man takes responsibility for himself; it was the very key to success. His father was not a man whose opinions were to be questioned in his own home, but Orion was already experienced enough to have seen tremendous hypocrisy in the adult world, so he secretly valued his own conclusions over those of all others. He did have gifts and he decided that his "knowing better" was one of them.

39.

Rufrak

"So then as far as you know he's never seen a horse before then?" Joan was on the phone asking Jeff about Rufrak. He had brought the dog home from college after a friend's bitch had ten pups and, following a summer in Virginia, it was clear to everyone Rufrak would be staying there.

"Well, I can't think of any time when he did in my company. Seems kinda weird that he never saw one there though, huh?"

"I suppose, but I think the Clarkes are the closest people around here with them and I've never seen anyone riding on our street."

"The poor guy must have been terrified," said Jeff.

It seemed the Fairchilds, Harvey Turner's neighbors, had purchased a horse for their oldest boy. Shortly before the Warrens' return, Harvey's ten-year-old, Tim, had brought the dog for a walk over to the Fairchilds' corral, unbeknownst to the other Turners. Rufrak had started crying and squirming and trying to back away, as soon as he spied the huge black beast. Tim had tried to grab his collar, but Rufrak nipped at him, an act which was totally out of character. The boy then took the dog's leash in both hands and tried to drag him closer to the horse, which scared Rufrak so badly he lost control of his bowels, before finally slipping his collar and bolting through the fence and down the road like a tiny fire storm.

"Harvey said the horse shattered Rufrak's belief system. He thought he'd already seen the biggest dogs there are!" Joan laughed.

She went on to tell him how Harvey said that dogs don't ask

for much for what they give us in return, unconditional love, companionship and protection, and the least we can do is to try to be as consistent with them as possible, because inconsistency confuses and scares them.

In this, dogs are not so unlike people. We all do a thing called "reality testing" all the time and when we encounter anything at all that doesn't appear to be consistent with what we believe to be reality, first we question it, then we question ourselves, but we remain confused and uncomfortable with it, until we either adjust our belief system, recognize where it actually fits into the original system, or go into a state of denial.

Harvey had picked up the dog to bring him to his place, when the Warrens last went to Santa Fe. Today Rufrak had been frightened at the sound of his arrival. He had slowly coxed the dog into his car with the plan of taking him and Tim, who had finally told his father about the event with the horse this morning, to a local ice cream stand and back, as a first step toward getting Rufrak past his newfound fears and mending his relationship with the boy. They hadn't returned yet.

"*A Course In Miracles* says that controversy is always available, but so is consistency," said Jeff. "When I think of how easily I can get involved in an argument, when I already have awareness of a higher truth, I sometimes think it might be easier to be a dog."

"Yes, but if you were a dog, you'd have been unable to read this course of yours!" Joan postulated.

"Ah yes, but I wouldn't need all the unlearning of meaningless words that 'The Course' is designed to take you through, either," Jeff replied.

40.

Flesh and Blood

"You've got to figure, that some people go out on the ocean and fish, because on land they have to be dealing with people," Berkley Dighton was enlightening Paul. "Not everyone *wants* a deckhand."

Paul was standing on a dock next to The Kal-Phee, the salmon trawler on which Sandra Callahan, number seven of the nine missing women, had been a deckhand before her disappearance, conversing with the boat's owner, as Dighton expertly used a razor sharp knife to clean one salmon after another. He slit them from anus to thorax, cut the throat latch, pulled down the head, tore out the gills and threw them over the side. He cleanly cut a circular path around the exposed inner throat, then he reached into the body cavity and pulled out all of the fish's guts in one piece and tossed them overboard. He flipped the knife over and used the scraper end to scrape out the length of the inner spine, then flipped it again and deftly removed the head, tossing it where the gills and guts had gone. He rinsed the fish with a hose, inside and out, and stacked it in a rapidly filling hopper with the bodies of the other fish that had already been eviscerated. The whole process took just over a minute.

"Me, I can have it either way. I'm comfortable alone, but I prefer good company. Sandra was good company, Mr. Warren. She was real good people and a born seawoman. Best deckhand I ever had. Learned fast. Worked fast. Never ruined a fish with a careless cut."

"You knew her pretty well?"

"Well, I knew her as well as you know someone you've fished with for most of a season. You do a lot of jabberin' over suppers in a season, if you're a personable type, and Sandra wasn't exactly secretive. I suppose I could tell you a good bit about her. Not her life story, but I believe I knew who she was."

"No boyfriend, right?" asked Paul, already knowing the answer.

"She was gay, Mr Warren, and not ashamed of it. She was a happy woman."

"Girlfriend?"

"No one serious since she moved up from San Fran. She was hoping it would work out eventually with someone she'd left behind there. Someone named Delilah. She talked about her a lot."

"Of course. I remember reading that name now." Paul had read about the girlfriend only this morning in a file at Juneau Police Headquarters. "You saw her for the last time the day before she went missing?"

"I saw her crossin' the Walmart parking lot, right over there." He pointed up the road to the store that was everywhere now. "She was comin' out an' I was goin' in to get groceries for the mornin'. We'd been in town for three days waiting for a spare part for the fish-hold freezer engine and I'd got it installed that afternoon. I said, 'See you at 4 A.M., Sandra. You all set?' and she said, 'You betcha, Berk' and she walked on and I went on inside and then in the morning, she never came down to the boat."

Dighton cut into a salmon's inner throat and nicked the creature's beating heart, which shot a squirt of blood so red it was black directly into his right eye. He let the fish rest in the wooden bracket he used to hold his fish while cleaning and placed the knife down next to that.

"Damn!" he reacted.

"Gotcha!" Paul smiled.

Dighton wiped his eye with his right sleeve, then pulled off his right rubber glove, reached in his pocket, retrieved a blue and white handkerchief and used it and the hose to fully clean his face.

"Revenge of the salmon," said Dighton.

"Never say 'die'," said Paul. "So, you have any ideas, Mr. Dighton?"

"Well, I've thought about it long and hard, sir. That I have. She didn't leave of her own free will. Of that I'm certain. Like I said, she wasn't the secretive type. She'd've told me, if there'd been a change of plans." He sighed deeply, sat back against the bow and looked up at Paul. "We're out here in wilderness country. Miles and miles of empty land and water. People loggin', huntin', boats comin' and goin' all the time. Fishing boats, ferries, tourists, people runnin' away from the lower forty-eight, not knowing it's a harder life here. What I'm saying is there's a lot of comin's an' goin's of roughnecked dudes all the time and some of 'em are as bad as can be. The guy on the next stool at the cafe could be a priest or a predator and how are you gonna know, 'ey? I've had occasional ideas, but nothing beyond not likin' the way somebody looks. Nothin' you could call a suspicion."

"Well, I thank you for your time, Captain." Paul handed the man his business card, which Dighton took between two bloody rubberized fingers and slipped into his flannel shirt pocket. "If you think of anything at all, would you send me an email and I'll get back to you?"

"Sure thing, Mr. Warren. Sorry I couldn't tell you more."

41.

Delilah's Song

Paul was almost to the street when he heard Dighton's voice behind him. "Mr. Warren!" he called and when Paul turned around, the salmon fisherman was scuffing his rubber boots along the dock. Paul grasped the rail at his right and walked back down the rolling ramp he'd been ascending, meeting Dighton a few yards from its lower end.

"I don't know if this will give you any insights. I'd think not, but you're the pro. She kept all her stuff in her room on shore, 'cept the gear she'd bring along on a trip, but a couple of months after she disappeared, I found this under the mattress of her bunk on the boat." He handed the ex-agent a well worn, folded, white business size envelope with the name Sandra printed on the front in blue ink. Inside was a folded piece of white lined notebook paper. Paul unfolded it.

It was a song lyric, hand-printed in blue ink with letters in light green highlighter, which Paul took to indicate the tune's chords, superimposed over the words, which read:

> Don't Be Afraid Of Loving
>
> Don't look for something that isn't there
> And look to yourself first for happiness
> Don't break your heart over one who won't care,
> When all the illusions are laid to rest

But don't be afraid of loving
The one who makes you feel good
And don't hesitate to give 'em
Everything you feel like you should
'Cause when you love someone, nothing else matters
And those who make you feel right will be few
Love is dif'rent for everyone
Some people turn and run
And some of 'em are gonna wanna love you

Be on your guard not to misjudge
Another person's way of living
Don't be too quick to misunderstand
Another person's way of giving
But still you gotta know how to recognize
When someone just don't want you around
Don't break your heart going crazy over someone
Who's only gonna put you down
But if you love someone, let nothing else matter
An' always try to make 'em feel right
And if you can't accept the love of one
Ever turn away and run,
Find out why... if it takes all your life

Delilah Robin 7/30/2003

When Dighton saw Paul turn the page over, he said, "This Delilah was something of a singer-songwriter and it was apparently a point of contention in their relationship that she wasn't making much of a living at it."

"Yeah?"

"Sandra didn't care, mind you. She thought a person should do what they love."

"I see."

"Trouble had to do with Delilah not believing she was at all outstanding at it and saying she didn't really love it at all, that it was just a skill, but that it was really her *only* skill."

"Ahh…"

"You know anything about music?" asked Dighton.

"I know what I like," answered Paul. "And I'm not sure what these chords would add to it, but the right melody can turn a run of the mill piece of advice into a theme for a love life, I suppose."

"That's true, I guess," said Dighton, nodding his head and appearing to believe it was, as he turned to shuffle back to his boat. "Well, good luck, Mr. Warren."

"Thanks, Cap'n. Thanks a lot."

As Paul was about to place the paper back in the envelope, he realized there was something stuck to the inside that turned out to be a dog-eared snapshot of a woman, with a guitar case in her hand, standing next to the driver's door of a vintage yellow Volkswagen Beetle. She had long curly blond hair and was barely as tall as the car. She was dressed in a short blue denim skirt and jacket, black tights, a black turtleneck sweater and black leather boots and was coyly grinning up at the camera. Paul was certain she was the cutest young lady he had ever seen. He suddenly ached to be at home with Joan in his arms.

42.

Narcissists and Psychopaths

"Sure, I know about this," said Captain Franklin D. Rhodes, head of the Alaska State Police Homicide Division, Frank to everyone except his adversaries. He was looking at the song lyric Paul had handed him. He had been the lead investigator on the missing persons cases and though he had an entire department to run now and Paul had no official status, Rhodes was a man who was committed on a level higher than the organization in which he worked. Fellow dedicated law enforcement professionals, including retired ones, would always be "brothers" first and he had been very generous with his time and sharing of information with Paul since their first meeting the previous morning, as evidenced by the fact that it was well after the time when Rhodes could have gone home with a clear conscience and he was showing no sign of wanting to depart. "Dighton called me up as soon as he found it. I stopped by and looked at it that same afternoon. He wanted to know if I wanted it for evidence or if I thought Delilah might want it, if it wasn't. I told him it wasn't and she wouldn't."

Paul looked at the man quizzically, so he continued. "You've read about this woman?" Paul nodded affirmatively. "How she said the press wouldn't leave her alone and they were only college roommates?"

"Sure."

"Okay, well that's not exactly the truth and neither is what Sandra Callahan told Dighton. I talked to Delilah Robin on the phone a good half a dozen times… and it's Delilah Robin Sears, by the way; she's married to a big time real estate developer, Jamie Sears, has been since shortly after her college graduation; but you know that already, I'm sure." Paul was nodding again. "Anyhow, between that and what I learned from one of our State Park Rangers, Sally Light Rain, Tlingit woman who knew Sandra, I think I've got the real picture."

"Which is?"

"Well, first, that she's apparently happily married and second, there's a child, a daughter, born the first year of the marriage, third, that they were roommates at Berkeley, but *not* just roommates, fourth, that Sandra wanted Delilah to leave her husband and let Sandra support her. Turns out Sandra had a trust fund, rich as Croesus, but Delilah insisted her experimentation with women was over, that she would always love Sandra but she was happy with her husband, that she wasn't really even bi-sexual after all, but what Delilah told me was that Sandra was delusional, that she was a classic narcissist and that once she got an idea in her head, there was no changing her mind, unless she wanted to change it. She said she ran away to Alaska, rather than face the truth in San Francisco."

"Uh-huh."

"Then she says, 'But that's love, isn't it?' very casually with a deep sigh, just like she thought that clarified everything and we were just talking about some whimsical old pal we had in common, who was still alive, just off chasing a dream somewhere. I can still hear it in her voice. Bothers me to this day more than just about anything in that whole group of cases."

"And she looks so sweet," said Paul looking at the snapshot.

"Okay, the song. The song was written about Delilah's *boyfriend*, when she was a junior in college, and this woman must be a real magnet for drama, because she herself described this character as a psychopath and the only person she ever went out with who she wished she'd never met."

"Really?"

"Really."

"Do you know his name?" asked Paul. "Has he been looked into?"

"I know his address. Name is Wolestone Lisari and he's been serving life in The Halawa Correctional Facility in Aiea, Hawaii since his meth lab blew up in August of 2004 and killed three of his neighbors, including two kids."

"Hmm." Paul was absentmindedly folding the page on which the lyric was written and staring off into space imagining what the scene Rhodes had just mentioned might have looked like. He figured this was leading nowhere, decided to shelve it for now and then remembered his agenda. "Alright. Well. I can't seem to find Arnold Washburn in town, the last woman's husband? I'd like to see him and their place."

"Oh yeah, I'm sorry. I should have thought to tell you earlier. If you don't have the address where they lived, I can give it to you off the top of my head, but he's not *in* town anymore," said Rhodes.

"No?"

"No. 'Bout six months after she went missing, the guy won the state lottery! Can you believe it? 'Bout seven million bucks. He said it was God's way of releasing his family from an environment that only brought them suffering now. He was a manager at one of the fish packing plants. Quit the next day. Sold the house, car, furniture, everything. Moved his kids back to where he was raised to start fresh."

"Which is where?"

"Amarillo, Texas."

He Could Have Done Anything

Amarillo, Texas! thought Paul, one hundred and fifty miles east on Route 40 of Santa Rosa, New Mexico. No way.

43.

Playing As A Winner

Orion was an enthusiastic game player. Very early in life, he learned to become very skilled at anything and everything in which he bothered to involve himself and to work hard at becoming better and better at it. When he played a game, he always played to win and to win fairly. And he did win.

If he encountered cheaters, even cheaters on his own team, his approach was always the same. He would deride them in front of everyone, attempting to embarrass them for not being able to win fairly and he'd give them a shove or punch them on the shoulder and warn them to stop cheating or go home. If they showed any opposition to this discipline, he'd kick their ass or go down trying and on the rare occasions when they would kick his ass, he'd put them on a little list in his head and not scratch them off it, until he had become strong enough to catch up with them and thoroughly trounce them. Ultimately, nobody who ever got put on the list would escape his wrath.

This would, of course, not by any means go unnoticed. By the time he was halfway through grammar school, he was accustomed to being afforded genuine respect by all who knew him, whether they actually liked him or not.

44.

Backdoor Bobby

"Hola?"

"Bobby?"

"Is this line secure?"

"Who do you think y'r talkin' to?"

"Sorry, Painter. Force of habit, manito. What's up?"

"I need a full watch and history. *All* travel and expenses. The best you can do."

"No problema." Backdoor Bobby sounded confident for the simple reason that he was the premiere expert on the face of the planet at what he did and both men knew it.

Bobby, whose real name was Pedro Fernandez, was a computer hacker. When the FBI finally busted the guy going by indianasantana, who they'd been relentlessly seeking for over a decade and through scores of aliases (they had nick-named him Backdoor Bobby, though he was using muchotoucho when they first caught wind of him, and being used to it, Paul had decided to use Bobby as his codename in private communications with Fernandez), they'd offered him a deal and put him to work on a full time basis. It kept him out of the slammer and under the microscope, paid well, offered him security and gave the Feds access to the cutting edge of hacking, while it allowed him to do what he most wanted to do: have fun meeting the challenge of getting in and out of other people's systems undetected, taking (and leaving) whatever he wanted. Plus it gave him hands-on access to the Bureau's supercomputers.

"Yeah, but I want you to understand right now that this guy will be looking for surveillance…"

"Who isn't?"

"Yes, but I mean he's expecting it, okay?"

"Okay."

"And the stuff we're really looking for won't be on any system that can be traced to him."

That stopped Bobby. Paul held the phone and waited. Bobby wasn't saying a word and Paul was sure he even heard the never-ending clicking of Bobby's keyboard cease. It was a good ten seconds before he heard it begin again simultaneously with Bobby saying, "No problema, man. Sooner or later, I can track him on video to whatever station he's doing his discreet on."

"Really?"

"Absolutely, bro! Gimme what you got. You know who he really is yet?"

"I know his name and address."

"Christ, this'll be easy!"

"Bobby?"

"Yes?"

"Take me seriously, now."

"Always, Paint; you know me…"

"This is *not* going to be easy. This guy is one of the smartest fucks who ever ran a con; do you understand me?"

"Si, jefe. I do."

"Okay. He's also dangerous. You'd spit in the eye of a Russian mobster, before you'd look at this guy cross-eyed, so you've got to do this completely undetected. Are we clear?"

"Of course, jefe."

"Alright. Now when I say history, I mean from birth and *family* history before that."

"This could take some time."

"Just feed it to me as you get it and call anything that seems to catch your eye to my attention."

"Like?"

"Like what stands out, seems wrong, seems too good to be true or you know from somewhere else isn't true. That especially."

"Okay."

"And this is strictly between you and me, comprende?"

"Si, comprende. What's the name, Paint?"

Paul gave him the name.

45.

Anomalies

The house where Paulette and Arnold Washburn had lived with their three kids, two dogs, a cat and two guinea pigs was a three bedroom cape on Evergreen Ave. with a small front yard and a big back yard. The neighboring houses were visible.

The most remarkable thing about the house, in Paul's estimation, was that it was painted white with green and red trim in an exact imitation of the colors of the flag of Bulgaria, which the current owner, a Ms. Maria Todorova, explained had been her intention and first order of business when she acquired the house from Arnold Washburn, who had been happy with it in barn red with white trim, as evidenced by the file photos Paul had seen.

Ms. Todorova was a petite, feisty, blonde, Bulgarian immigrant, who had left behind a career as a singer to come to Alaska six years earlier and become a nurse. She was proud to say that very recently she had also become an American citizen. Paul estimated her age to be around forty and would have been surprised to learn that he was short by a decade and that this was a testament to what a complete absence of laziness can do. He thought she had a very matter of fact manner and a charming accent, in which she explained that she had never met the previous owner, that his real estate agent had handled the deal, that there had been no haggling over the low bid she had offered and that she had heard every rumor under the sun about the disappearance of Paulette Washburn, but had drawn no conclusions herself, except that most of them were, of course, incorrect. She was clearly more interested in explaining that now that she was an American, she was intending to change the green trim to the blue of the American flag.

She told Paul he could feel free to look around and proceeded to give him a tour of the entire house, then left him to examine the rest of the property on his own. It all told him exactly nothing.

In fact, the only thing he felt was significant about the place he knew as soon as he realized where it was located. It was far to the south of where every other missing woman had lived or worked and Paul was aware that this was not the only anomaly in the case of Paulette Washburn.

Others included the fact that she was the only one who had been living with her husband at the time she vanished, though four others had been married, both dancers and the bartender, who were divorced, and the waitress, who had been living with her new boyfriend while finalizing a divorce. Mrs. Washburn was also the only one who had been living with her kids, though one of the dancers had a ten-year-old son living in Salinas, California with her mother and the cashier had a four-year-old living with his dad in Ketchikan, Alaska. Mrs. Washburn was the only woman missing who had no job outside of the home, including the college freshman, Amy Waterbury, who had worked as a chambermaid at The Potlach Inn in her hometown of Sitka, until days before she disappeared and though it couldn't be said for certain when Amy vanished, Paulette Washburn was the only one of the nine women who definitely went missing during the daylight hours. Her three kids all got off the same school bus shortly after three in the afternoon and within minutes discovered that she was not at home. Also, when Paul had examined the photographs of all nine women, he felt there was something different about Paulette Washburn that he couldn't quite put his finger on, but he thought he saw in her eyes that there was something behind them that she didn't want anyone to see.

Paul was beginning to get a hunch or two and he wanted to talk to Captain Rhodes again, but first he wanted to know what Backdoor Bobby had learned thus far.

46.

Church

"This guy Biggleston says that six of them all attended church on Glacier Highway," said Paul to Captain Rhodes between bites of a delicious fresh halibut fillet. He and Rhodes were having lunch at the captain's insistence at his favorite luncheon spot, Rick's Cafe. Paul understood clearly why it was Rhodes' favorite: no frills, friendly service, great food and plenty of it.

Edgar Biggleston was a reporter for *The Juneau Mariner*, the city's oldest and most widely circulated newspaper. He had achieved celebrity status locally during the time of the disappearances, staying on the cutting edge of the story, but his information was always accurate and all of his columns were included in their own file amended to the case files of each of the missing women.

"That's a fact," said Rhodes, "All except the first one, the first dancer, Joselyn Bonica, who was not a church goer, and the last two, Waterbury and Washburn. Waterbury was new to town and would probably have started attending mass at the Catholic church close to campus, but hadn't yet and Paulette Washburn and family were regulars at the Christian Science Church on Calhoun Ave. But you've seen Glacier Highway; it's one of the longest thoroughfares in Juneau, with a whole lot of churches."

"Yeah, but you have to admit that, statistically, it's outstanding that eight out of nine were even regular churchgoers. And given the number of churches in Juneau that aren't on Glacier Highway, it seems like it could be meaningful, were it not for the other three."

"Well, you said you wanted to see something in the geography. I guess it could be something. You can run computer models on just the six and see if it gives you anything interesting," suggested Rhodes.

"Yeah, I'm gonna do that," said Paul, already picturing it in his mind's eye. "I think I've seen everything I can see here, unless that really shows me something. I'll be leaving in the morning."

"Well, don't be too disappointed. I lived and breathed this stuff every day and I may not have all of your skills, but I'm no slouch either and… here we are."

"I'm not really disappointed, Frank. I haven't solved your disappearances, but I still think something is going to gel. Sometimes you even know things already that you just haven't realized are answers, you know?"

"Sure, happens all the time."

"Listen Frank, I know you never found any proof, but, gut feeling… was Paulette Washburn fooling around?"

Rhodes put his fork on his plate, placed both hands on the edge of the table, looked Paul squarely in the eye and said, "Gut feeling, based on how hard her husband fought the idea mostly, nothin' I ever confirmed or even heard before the rumor mill had been churning about her a good while… yeah. Yeah, my guess would be she was."

47.

Compartmentalization

An organizational skill that is often seen in organized serial predators is the ability to separate that aspect of their lives from what is observed by those around them by means of emotional detachment or disassociation from the thoughts and acts involved in their crimes.

Some among this type of perpetrator are so successful at it that those who have lived in closest proximity to them, their family, friends and/or co-workers, are never able to reconcile their experience of the person they thought they knew with the person who the authorities have brought to justice. It's not, in fact, uncommon for a multiple personality disorder defense to be proposed with this type of criminal, though it rarely applies and is even less often successful, because most folks on the prosecution's side of things know that what they are dealing with is somebody with the ability to compartmentalize.

Compartmentalization may sound cold to many of us and it seems a pure impossibility to those at the other end of the spectrum, obsessive-compulsives and the like, but it's actually taught in business management and self-empowerment courses, among others, as a way of prioritizing and sticking to priorities, because of its proven effectiveness. We all multitask, but we're also all familiar with the concept of concentrating fully on one thing at a time. Those who are best at compartmentalization can literally put out of their minds that which need not be dealt with now and leave it there until it is time to deal with it. It's a powerful tool.

48.

Avoidance Behaviors

Micky Landis was a twenty-seven-year-old carpet cleaner from Zachary, Louisiana, maybe half an hour's drive on Route 19 north from Baton Rouge. He'd lived there his whole life and everyone knew him. Anyone whose carpets he had ever cleaned would have been happy to recommend him to anyone who had spilled grape juice on their beige dining room rug or whose dog had had "an accident" on an heirloom.

Micky liked working alone with his noisy machines in other people's houses, because it allowed him to spy on them and their neighbors, while keeping them from trying to converse with him beyond a necessary minimum. Micky had a severe stutter as a child and though he had managed to conquer it with the help of a speech therapist whose specialty was helping children with that exact problem, an inner terror, not of pitifully stammering with no control other than to stop attempting to speak, as he once had, but of getting stuck just enough to draw attention and then derision, motivated him to avoid having to speak with anyone. Avoidance behaviors had, for most of his life, dominated his social skills.

"One thing leads to another" is what Micky often said to himself and he was no dummy. But the other kids were merciless when he was a boy. They'd say mean things like: "You have Zachary's disease. You talk Zachary like I fart!" Oh, how he'd hated them all! They thought they were funny, but they were all just stupid. He was the smart one and they'd never know it, because they'd never get to know what was going on inside his head.

"Nobody ever knows what's going on inside your head unless you tell them" was another thing Micky liked to say to himself. He was no dummy. He knew that he knew what psychologists know: you can only observe behavior, not thoughts, not the motivation behind behavior.

So Micky kept his observable behavior within the range of socially acceptable acts, stayed, with his thoughts, safely behind the barrier his machines provided during work hours and spent most of his free time alone. He didn't like people who were still alive.

49.

Shiv

Paul was standing in the hallway of the courthouse in Las Vegas, Nevada with Harvey Turner and Shirley McAdams, the mother of the murdered girl. Now there was a commotion in the mass of people behind him in the hall. Apparently the paperwork had been completed and Andrew Travis Johansen was about to join them in the hallway. Paul was suddenly terrified and he knew he knew why and knew just as clearly that he wouldn't be able to do anything about the reason why, because somehow whatever it was had already happened and he suddenly thought the feeling of defeat that accompanied this realization was more than he could bear. He began to turn toward the commotion and he caught Harvey's eyes widening as he looked past Paul at whatever it was. This scared him even more and he tried to turn faster, but felt like he was moving under water against the force of the stifling humidity and his inner awareness of the futility of trying.

As he completed his turn, out of the fifty or sixty people in that part of the hall, reporters extending microphones and beginning to shout questions, lights and TV cameras, and although the man was among those farthest away from him, Paul immediately focused on Tom McAdams. Tom's attention, like that of everyone around him, seemed to be riveted on Andrew Travis Johansen, and as he closed the distance between himself and his daughter's murderer, Paul was sure, from the look on his face, he needed to be stopped. Paul started to shout, knowing it wouldn't help and he saw Tom McAdams lunge at Andrew Travis Johansen from behind. Tom's left hand grabbed Johansen's hair and his right hand, which held the broken off, plastic handle from a men's room paper towel dispenser, in an instant came over the man's right shoulder, the makeshift blade found the left side of the man's neck and Tom slashed his throat deeply from left to right in one stroke.

Now everything seemed to be happening in slow motion. Paul saw the horror and amazement in those closest to the spray of blood from Andrew Travis Johansen's jugular veins and virtually everyone in that part of the hallway not holding a TV camera or too stunned to move jumping on Tom McAdams. Paul, still moving towards McAdams, began to rotate his head and upper body to the left to glance back at Mrs. McAdams, at Harvey, at Phillip and Andrea Smithson, but the phone on the table next to his motel bed rang before he could complete his turn. He lay there while it rang twice more, perspiring, breathing hard and staring bug-eyed at a corner of the room where two walls met the ceiling, then reached for the telephone receiver.

50.

Clue

The call was from Edgar Biggleston, the reporter from *The Juneau Mariner*. Paul had called his office the previous evening and, finding him away for the night, had left a message. Biggleston had called immediately after arriving at work and then apologized for waking Paul, who in turn thanked him for the wake-up call, explaining that he had a plane to catch in a few hours.

He told Biggleston that he'd called to ask if the reporter could give him any information about the Washburn couple's Christian Science faith. Had he learned anything from other church members, for instance, and specifically, did he have any idea how deeply committed they were?

"Funny you should ask," replied Biggleston. "She was the one who brought him to the church. He was some kind of Protestant back in Texas, but I can tell you without fear of contradiction, Mr. Warren, this woman wore the pants in the family."

"Really?"

"Oh, yeaah! Everybody, without exception, told me that."

"Uh-huh. Well thanks, Mr. Biggleston…"

"Please: Ed."

"Thank-you for calling, Ed…"

"Hey, listen! What's up? You must think you're onto something here. I mean this was never a federal case, because there was no proof of kidnapping or serial murder, but you must be here because you're fairly well convinced that it should have been, am I right?"

Under the circumstances, Paul saw no problem in admitting that he believed they were dealing with a serial murderer. They talked for several minutes about the missing women before Biggleston confirmed something that Franklin Rhodes had touched on, that Amy Waterbury's parents calls to the policeman hadn't ceased, until he moved to the State Police homicide division and the cold case was put in the hands of others. Biggleston told Paul that by that time George and Henrietta Waterbury, mainly Henrietta, had been calling him, as well, for nearly as long as Rhodes and their calling had continued like clockwork, on the third of every month, the third being the last day on which anyone could say they had seen Amy, until last month, when they hadn't called, and now it had been almost seven weeks since they had spoken.

"I've been thinking about calling them, in fact, but I'm wondering if maybe they've finally reached the acceptance stage of their grief," explained the reporter.

"Maybe they have, Ed," offered Paul.

They spoke a while longer. Paul gave the reporter his contact information and asked him to be in touch if he learned or thought of anything at all that he sensed might be relevant, Biggleston wished him a good trip home and they said their good-byes, but Paul was thinking the entire time about how it's that which is out of place, like a break in a pattern, a clockwork-like succession of phone calls, for instance, that constitutes a clue.

He picked up the receiver again. He was still going to be flying, but he wasn't going home.

51.

Q & A

M ost people will answer a direct question. Not everyone will speak the truth when asked, but an experienced detective will usually sense the difference between deception and accuracy. How one asks, where and when one asks a question are often the keys to success. Having a good idea in advance of what the correct answer is can obviously be a great advantage.

Things were beginning to coalesce in Paul's mind, so much so that he had to remind himself not to become overly confident in what he was now pretty sure was the truth about Amy Waterbury, and, if he was correct, what it might mean in respect to his solving the case of all of the Juneau disappearances, until he was certain about the answers to a few more specific questions.

At this point, however, Paul needed an answer to a question he was asking himself and he needed a little help, so he called Captain Rhodes for his expert opinion about Mr. and Mrs. Waterbury. Rhodes, who had seen and heard his share of the unbelievable, was at first a bit surprised by what Paul theorized, but after a brief explanation he thought that if Paul could get George Waterbury on the phone, the man would be honest with him and it wouldn't be necessary to fly to Sitka and add the intimidation factor of an in person interview, so for the sake of economy and expedience, Paul's next call was to the Waterbury home.

"Mr. Waterbury?"

"Yes?"

"Mr. Waterbury, my name is Paul Warren. I'm a former special agent with the Federal Bureau of Investigation, currently working with Captain Frank Rhodes (it wasn't really a lie) on the case of the Juneau disappearances."

There was a moment's hesitation, before George Waterbury said, "Yes?"

"Mr. Waterbury, I spoke with Edgar Biggleston a half an hour ago and he told me that your wife and yourself have been in the habit of calling him quite regularly every month, until last month, and that it's now been an unusually long time since he's heard from either of you," said Paul and when he thought he heard George Waterbury draw a breath, he believed the man was trying to think of just how to begin to explain, so he took the plunge. "Mr. Waterbury, have you heard from Amy?"

52.

Developments

It was no surprise to Paul that George and Henrietta Waterbury had indeed heard from their daughter. Mr. Waterbury explained that they had been embarrassed to admit they'd learned she had run off on the day of her disappearance, first to Montreal and then to Southern France, with a young man she had met and fallen in love with during her college orientation weekend, which had been late in June of that year. George Waterbury made it clear that they would not have approved of this romance and, from their conversation, Paul surmised that Amy had been subjected to a rather parochial upbringing by parents to whom she had been born an only child, when they were in their late forties. Amy had, after all, used her going away to school as an opportunity to flee from them and begin a whole new, less restricted life. Whether she had ever intended to contact her parents again would remain a mystery. She still had no intention of returning from Europe, but she had recently given birth to a child of her own, a daughter, and she had sent them a photograph of the newborn along with a short, unapologetic letter of explanation the previous month, which Mr. Waterbury could confirm was definitely in her handwriting.

He said they were going to call and explain what had happened and said he was awfully sorry that he hadn't already and sorrier still for all the trouble Amy had caused and asked Paul if they or their daughter might be in yet more trouble for withholding information.

Paul told the man he didn't believe they would be, that he was glad that they had learned she was alive and well and that the authorities would be relieved that they could at least close her case. He told him they'd probably be hearing from someone shortly in order to officially confirm the authenticity of the letter, but that, although Amy deserved a good scolding, none of them had anything to fear from the law.

"I'll be damned," was Captain Rhodes reaction when Paul called and informed him of this development.

"I'm not a religious man, but I doubt it," replied Paul. "Besides I've got a pretty good idea about something else that's going to come as even more of a surprise to you."

"Oh yeah? What's that?"

"Well, it's about Arnold Washburn. I've got a computer hacker on the payroll at the Bureau, who does some work for me as well, from time to time, and I've had him do some checking up on him. What he's given me leads me to believe you're going to want to bring him back to Alaska."

53.

Gallows Humor

"This is a nation of laws and the system works. There's a couple of myths for you!" exclaimed Andy Everly to the friends at his table at Mastro's, the Beverly Hills steakhouse where they'd all gone for dinner after he'd "killed" at the Laugh Factory earlier in the evening. "This is a nation of lawbreakers and victims and if your car or your computer worked as well as the legal system, you'd bring it right back where you bought it and demand your money back!"

"But would you get it?" asked Jeff Warren, who'd come to town to supervise the delivery and installation of his A Course In Miracles sculpture at the Los Angeles County Museum of Art, where Oprah Winfrey had decided it should spend some time being admired by the general public. "I mean, considering that the legal system is broken and all?"

"Is it still under warranty?" asked Justine King.

"Are we talking about a car or a computer?" asked Barry Fine.

"It doesn't matter what we're talking about. Everything is broken!" answered Andy. "Just like the Dylan song! Everything in this whole fucking country, ever since Bush got elected, everything that wasn't broken has been broken and most of it by him and his cronies! Goddamn moron! I'll tell you something: I predict he'll be the first president to be assassinated after leaving office. Some Iraq war veteran…"

"Now Andy, not everyone is going to know you're joking…,"

Barry began to admonish him, glancing around to see who might have heard.

"I'm not joking!" insisted Andy. Then he lowered his voice a decibel. "I'm not advocating it. I'm just predicting it. You'll remember when he first announced his candidacy, that I predicted if he were to be elected, it would turn out to be the worst thing that ever happened to this country and I've predicted just about every disaster we've suffered ever since, except for exactly what the catalyst would be that turned out to be 9/11. Well, once again, I'm telling you: mark my words."

"You haven't said this on stage, have you, buddy?" asked Jeff.

"No, I told you: this isn't a joke," Andy replied.

"Good, because it isn't funny," said Barry.

"No, but it would give a lot of people who've been harmed by his idiocy the last laugh," Andy retorted, glaring at his agent. "How much is your house worth today, by the way? You realize that regardless of the conditions that existed before the turnaround in the housing market, it was Bush who caused the turnaround by threatening to do away with the mortgage interest income tax deduction to help pay off his deficit, don't you? And the media hasn't said one word about that. Not one word anywhere."

Barry didn't answer.

"Wasn't the real estate market already slowing down?" asked Justine.

"The real estate market was still healthy and growing; that was part of Bush's reasoning for doing away with the deduction; though they were doing things like running week-long specials on TV like 'Is The Bubble Going To Burst?' in an effort to slow it down. My condo was still appreciating at better than twelve percent."

"Who's 'they'?" asked Justine.

Andy ignored the question and said, "Hey, speaking of veterans and everything being broken, here's something I want to know and it's pretty damn relevant too, considering that we're in the middle of another war that a whole lot of us predicted would be another Vietnam and is: how come veterans who have been on the wrong side of an issue get preferential treatment in the job market? My dad has been a conscientious objector since 1971. Do you think he ever made out a job application that asked him if he was in the anti-Vietnam war movement? Of course not. And he's one hell of a lot smarter than anyone who went over there."

"Did my wife write that?" asked Jeff.

"She might have," answered Andy. "She's smart enough to at least agree with me. And that's really the point. The public education system is intentionally broken, so that there's always an enormous supply of young people who are stupid enough to think that the military offers them opportunities... opportunities like the education they didn't get in the public schools. Don't think there's no connection between America being number one militarily, but only number thirteen educationally. It's all part of the same plan."

"I'm sure Alvina has said that," said Jeff, "And there's certainly nothing in the budget with which you could dispute it."

"Well, at least the price of oil is still dropping," offered Justine.

"But the price of gasoline is going up again!" cried Andy. "How the fuck does *that* work?"

54.

Whoever Speaks First…

"I knew you'd be here for me eventually," were the first words out of Arnold Washburn's mouth when he answered the door of his home in Amarillo the next morning. He hadn't seen the rented black Crown Victoria pulling up his driveway, but he didn't seem to be particularly surprised to see Frank Rhodes standing with Paul just outside of his front door, when he opened it, after they'd rung his doorbell twice. He looked Captain Rhodes straight in the eye, looking supremely tired, and he actually smiled faintly and, nodding his head, said, "In fact it's a relief… it feels like a relief… that you've finally come. Now I can stop worrying. Come in. Come in."

They came in, Paul closing the door behind him. He saw they were in a large, well furnished living room, with wooden walls which were made to look like a rustic ranch in a style that Texans and other westerners are often fond of. He could see family pictures on the wall by the stone fireplace, including a large photo-real painting of a serenely smiling Paulette Washburn hanging over the mantel, with a glow about her head meant to suggest that now she was in heaven.

Arnold Washburn asked, "Is it alright if I sit down?", and he did so. The two lawmen remained silently standing. This was the plan. So far, things were proceeding precisely as Paul had predicted they would. From what Backdoor Bobby had told him, he knew the man was suffering from a nervous condition, had an ulcer and never seemed to leave the house except to attend regular church services. Washburn had returned to the Presbyterian faith of his youth. Bobby had also supplied the information that Washburn had never served in he military, nor was there anything indicating he was a hunter.

He noticed Paul looking at his deceased wife's portrait and said, "She's not in heaven, you know. She was an adulteress, an unrepentant one, and she's... she's gone to... she's gone to the other place." He looked down at the floor and shook his head. Rhodes thought for a moment that he might cry, but he didn't. He went on, "I knew right away I shouldn't have killed her, but from the instant I found out that she was going to leave me for the man... the man she was cheating with...," and now he did sob, "I just couldn't stop myself!"

Now Captain Rhodes and Paul took chairs opposite Washburn, but still they said nothing.

Washburn looked at Captain Rhodes and explained, "From the time I met her, I gave her everything she ever wanted, no matter what it was, no matter how hard I had to work to afford it. I never denied her a thing. It wasn't always easy, but I didn't mind. I loved her. I loved her so much." He shook his head and looked as if he were trying to understand why his love hadn't resulted in a life of happiness ever after. "So I gave her whatever she wanted and did whatever she said she wanted us to do, move to Alaska, have another child. Those were her ideas, her wishes." He sighed, deeply. "But Paulette was someone who was always thinking that the next thing would make her happy and always finding that it didn't. Have you ever known that type of person, Lieutenant Rhodes?"

Now that the man had confessed, Rhodes was willing to answer. "Yes, Mr. Washburn, I have. It's Captain Rhodes now, by the way, and I work for Alaska State Police Homicide. But yes, I've seen many people with that same problem."

"Yes," said Washburn and he sighed again. "Many people never learn... never learn to appreciate what they have. You know, I felt sorry for her... always felt sorry for her that she was that way, but the only thing I knew how to do was to try to satisfy her... and then I lost control... and then... as soon as she was dead, I felt sorry for her again." He looked from one man to the other and back again, as if to see if they believed him.

"I think I understand, Mr. Washburn," said Rhodes.

"But I had to think of the kids," explained Washburn, "So I... hid... I hid what I'd done and pretended I didn't know anything."

Rhodes nodded silently and waited.

"I suppose you want to know what I did with her... with her...," and now Washburn broke down crying, remembering whatever it was he had done with his wife's body. He clutched at his ulcerated stomach, jumped up and quickly retrieved a brass wastebasket that stood next to a nearby, antique, roll-top desk and, having fallen to his knees, retched over it. After a while he stood and apologized, wiping his mouth with a handkerchief. "I have an terrible ulcer. Of course, I deserve it."

"I see," said Rhodes. "Now, Mr. Washburn..."

"You're going to want to take me back to Juneau," Washburn anticipated being told, once more looking from one man to the other and back again. "I won't fight it. I want to go with you. I want all of this to be over. I'll be glad when all of this is... when all of this is just over. I swear to you, I feel like a weight has been lifted off of me already."

55.

Complete Pictures

Now that it had been confirmed that the Waterbury and Washburn women were not factors in the puzzle, Paul was happy to have in his company the man who had originally been in charge of the missing persons cases. As they rode to the airport with Arnold Washburn, he inquired of Captain Rhodes, who was driving, "Frank, do you recall if there were any missing persons cases of men between the ages of twenty and forty that occurred at the same time as Sandra Callahan's disappearance?"

Rhodes barely had to give it a thought. He replied, "Well, in fact there was a guy whose father began looking for him the same day that she was reported missing: Steven Beck, twenty-seven; father was a minister at the Salvation Army. He was frantic, 'cause his son was barely ever absent from home or the church and retreat center. A real loner. Nice fellow, by all reports. Shy, but helpful to the folks who came around. Never surfaced again. Father died about eighteen months later. Buried in their cemetery."

"They have their own cemetery?"

"Not a big one, but they bury a good number of people there who pass away without having had the means for other arrangements."

"What was Steven's occupation?" asked Paul.

"Well, he worked for his father; pretty much everything that didn't require a lot of smarts that wasn't being handled by one of the other administrators or volunteers. Not a very bright boy apparently, but he did maintenance, house cleaning, landscaping of the properties, dug the occasional grave…"

"He dug the graves?"

"That's what his father said."

Paul looked out the window and, though his eyes saw the terrain and the buildings they were passing, his inner vision imagined a cemetery coming into focus like a developing photograph. He liked to say that developing photographs were metaphoric of the way all the elements of a case would sometimes suddenly come together to give one a complete picture.

Paul reached down into the bag at his feet and retrieved his laptop. He said to Rhodes, "You know, I plotted a good number of grids the other night with just the six church goers and with the first seven women and since we don't know just exactly where they were taken from, I had to work with other factors: homes, places of employment, where they attended Sunday services mainly. Naturally that tended to cluster the results in that same Glacier Highway area. I don't recall where the Salvation Army church is…"

"The administration and church offices are on West Willoughby, but the retreat center is right off Glacier Highway at Seven Mile Road," Rhodes enlightened him, "And they administer to about ten different locations in the area."

Paul had saved all of the Juneau grids in his computer and could now see on his screen that the location of the Salvation Army Retreat Center was just southeast of an area that many of the grids he'd plotted had centered on.

"You said West Willoughby? Is that road? Street?" he asked.

"West Willoughby Ave. It's in the five hundred block, even side of the street. South side."

Paul was nearly certain he'd have a difficult time holding a satellite signal for Google Earth in the moving car, but gave it a try anyhow. For the moment, he got lucky and saw that the church and administration offices were just southwest of an area that the remainder of his grids had indicated were a probable hotspot.

"Well Frank, I think we've got a winner."

"Yeah?"

"I'm gonna want to see this cemetery as soon as we get back."

Though Arnold Washburn, in the back seat, had his own problems to think about, so far it had proved to be quite an educational ride for him.

56.

Tactile Memory

"Don't you find that every woman is different?" Orion asked.

"More or less," his old friend, Gary Knayler, agreed noncommittally.

"More or less," said Orion, shaking his head. The two men were having a late lunch in The Sky Lounge, a restaurant which overlooked the small airfield where they had spent the latter part of the morning and early afternoon with Knayler teaching Orion to fly a Robinson R44 helicopter. Gary had taught the man to fly a plane shortly after they had come home from the Vietnam war, but helicopters were a whole different animal.

Helicopters don't actually fly. The disc that is the spinning top rotor flies. The rest of the machine hangs from the disc while the pilot keeps the whole craft in balance using both hands and both feet. Some skilled airplane pilots are never able to manage the transition to helicopters and it's frequently argued that it might be easier to learn to fly a helicopter, if you've never flown a plane, just as calculus is often easiest learned by children who haven't already acquired extensive skills in Euclidean mathematics. "I'm not talking about slight differences, Bird." Bird was the war-name Knayler had earned in the Nam. "I mean every woman is distinctly different in bed. And I'm not just talking about behavioral preferences. In fact, that's not what I mean at all. I'm talking about what they feel like, what they *taste* like and as a result how *I'm* different with every one of them."

"*Were* different," corrected Knayler.

"Of course." Orion was a well known advocate of monogamy for partners in committed relationships and, being married, there was no question regarding his fidelity to his wife. "But there's nothing wrong with my memory and besides, I'm asking about you now. The miracle is that I found one woman with whom I could be satisfied to the point that I could forgo all the rest of them. You know how easily I become disinterested in things once I'm familiar with 'em. But let me give you a good example of what I'm talking about. Do you remember the Lee twins?"

"Karen and Sharon. You called them Carin' and Sharin'. How could I forget? Beautiful girls! Always smiling. Hair down to their asses..."

"That's them. Well then you may have assumed this, but I was sleeping with both of them most of that spring in Winterhaven and those girls were absolutely *identical* from head to toe. They hardly knew each other apart, finished each other's sentences, the whole bit. But, Bird, I'm telling you, I could tell which one was which when I was makin' it with them. And it was incredible to me, because their skin was the same and they did everything the same way! They kissed the same and their mouths tasted alike; I couldn't tell them apart when they went down on me, but when I was in either one of 'em, I knew which one she was. And I'll tell you somethin' else: if I was stone blind, I believe I could identify all the women I've ever been with, just by what they feel like."

"Does your wife know about this, Sport?" asked Knayler.

"Now why in the world would I tell my wife such a thing?"

"I think you're gonna make a good chopper pilot, Sport."

57.

Orion's Wife

Orion's wife was the most self-confident and capable woman he'd ever met. He'd have preferred to have her watching his back than some of the men he'd been with in the jungles of Vietnam. She was a judo expert and a crack shot with a pistol, rifle or shotgun, but could not be equaled in the use of the antique Colt Buntline revolver, with its 14 inch barrel, that her father had left her.

She turned the heads of all who gazed upon her, was tall and slender with dark brown eyes, an arresting smile and long, jet black hair. "Mesmerizingly beautiful" is how a local magazine article about her city's ten most successful women had described her.

It was said that she looked exactly like her mother, Flame Two Trees, a full-blooded Apache, who had died giving birth to her. Her father had been a professional gambler named Wild Bill Burnright. He had raised her all by himself, teaching her everything he knew, before being shot to death one roastingly hot, Texas night in Abilene by a drunken cowboy, who had just lost a month's wages to him on the turn of a card. At the time, she was only ten years old and she'd spent the next four years in an orphanage before running away to San Francisco, where she'd lived among the hippies of the Haight Ashbury district for two years and then returned to Texas to reclaim the ranch her father had left her just north of Sweetwater.

Wild Bill's game had been five card stud poker and legend had it that you didn't sit down at the table with him unless you could afford to lose. His daughter had followed in his footsteps, though she'd turned to Texas hold 'em when it became wildly popular and had become one the world's top hands at it by the time she built the casino where she met Orion on the night of its grand opening. They fell hard for each other right off the bat.

They were a perfect match. Orion loved competition and beautiful, smart, strong women. She loved strong, intelligent, handsome men who were fierce competitors. They married only months later and, though Orion had majored in business and mass communication at one of the country's top schools, as the years went by, he was proud enough of her savviness to claim she'd taught him everything he knew about making deals out west. They were envied and admired by all, as they grabbed the world by the horns and wrestled it to submission.

She was the only person in the world to ever learn all of Orion's secrets and he was the only person that she ever told about her having killed a pimp in San Francisco, who had beaten her up, raped her and tried to turn her out on the street to trick for him, before she fled back to Sweetwater.

58.

"Please come home"

Returning to Juneau involved flying first to Seattle and changing planes. The first flight out wasn't until mid-afternoon, so Paul and Frank decided having a late lunch would be the best way to kill the time. They'd been dining for fifteen minutes when Paul's cell phone rang. He could see from the caller ID that it was Joan calling. He pushed the send button and put the phone to his ear as he swallowed a mouthful of barbecued pork.

"Hi babe. What's up?"

"Oh Paul…" Joan was clearly distraught. Paul knew immediately she was looking for the words to tell him something had happened, something very bad.

"What Joanie? What is it?"

"Oh Paul," she sobbed, "It's Harvey. He's had a terrible accident. He's in a coma."

"What? What happened? Is he going to be alright?"

She was choking on her tears now and didn't answer.

"Joanie. Honey, take a deep breath."

Paul heard his wife collecting herself. Finally she said, "He came and got Rufrak this afternoon. On the way to his house his SUV rolled over. He's on a ventilator, Paul…"

"My God, Joan, how…," and now it was he who found he couldn't go on.

"They don't know. They don't know what caused it. They don't know if he's going to make it, Paul!"

"Oh Jesus."

"Paul, please come home."

Paul looked at Frank Rhodes, who had stopped eating. He saw that both the police captain and Arnold Washburn, who understandably had no appetite, were watching him with sympathetic anticipation. He said, "I will, honey."

The situation may have been more complicated, had Washburn not been so willing to return to Alaska, but under the circumstances Rhodes was confident that he could handle everything without assistance and when Paul explained to him what had happened, he insisted that Paul fly directly home. Though the airport had the normal mid-day crowd, after twenty minutes Paul was able to exchange his ticket without a problem. Then the two detectives agreed that Rhodes would contact the current Salvation Army head administrator about checking their records for burials that closely coincided with the disappearances of the missing women.

"I wish I could be there with you, Frank, and see just what we're dealing with there, but unless I'm very mistaken, you're going to find that those women are buried in that cemetery," Paul told the homicide man.

"I'm sure you're not," agreed Rhodes, shaking his head.

Paul saw them to their security check point. Rhodes said he hoped Paul's ex-partner would be alright, that he'd be in his prayers. Paul thanked him, said he'd be calling him soon, they said their goodbyes and then Paul found his way to his own gate where he waited and wondered, if he wasn't mistaken, why had Orion not left Steven Beck's body where it and at least some evidence of one of the missing women would be immediately discovered.

59.

Wendy Cartwright's Eye

One day, shortly after Micky Landis had concluded the therapy for his stuttering, he was playing with Wendy Cartwright in her back yard when she asked him to go in the house with her to see if her mom would give them a couple of Popsicles. He agreed enthusiastically and quickly followed her toward the back door of the Cartwrights' house.

Wendy ran to the three back stairs, stepped up and swung the screen door open and, instead of proceeding inside, turned back to say something just as Micky reached up to grab the door, which was connected to the door jamb by a spring and in the process of swinging closed. She turned in such a way that the heel of his reaching right hand hit her squarely in her right eye causing her to scream in pain and run inside wailing at the top of her lungs. He ran in after her, of course, and found her bawling in her mother's arms and shrieking, between gasps, that he had punched her in the eye.

Amid Wendy's cries, each of which seemed to be louder and more agonized than the one which preceded it, and Mrs. Cartwright's questions, directed at both Wendy and Micky, the boy objected to Wendy's claim that he had punched her, said she hadn't been looking and it had been an accident caused by her turning around as he was reaching for the door.

The two children had always gotten along well and Mrs. Cartwright looked like she wanted to believe Micky, but Wendy continued to scream and cry hysterically and insist he'd punched her and she wailed until no sound came from her little mouth until, finally, Mrs. Cartwright decided, to Micky's relief, that it would be best for him to go home and explain to his mother what had happened. He said, "Okay," then he said, "I'm sorry; but it was an accident," and he departed.

Micky went right home and found his mother in the kitchen on the telephone. She looked at him with a scowl, pointed at a kitchen chair and said, "Sit there." He sat in the chair and waited, wishing he could hear what Mrs. Cartwright was telling his mother and able to guess from his mother's responses that the other woman hadn't concluded whether or not the incident had been accidental. After what seemed like a long time, but, because Mrs. Cartwright still had an injured, crying child to attend to, was actually only a few minutes, Micky's mother hung up the phone.

"What did you do to Wendy Cartwright?" she demanded.

"It was an accident!" Micky insisted and he proceeded to explain what had happened, while his mother questioned him about each detail and he explained some more. She wasn't happy about it, to say the least, but finally she seemed satisfied that he was telling her the truth and she told him to sit right where he was until she got back, went down the hall to the large den, scooped his little brother Timmy up from within his playpen and returned. She told him not to get out of that chair, as she passed through the kitchen, and with the three-year-old in her arms, left by the back door.

When she returned, some twenty minutes later, she looked even less pleased than when she had left. She put Timmy back in his playpen, came in the kitchen, pulled a chair from under the table, rotated his chair to face hers and sat down.

"That little girl's eye is swollen out to here!" she exclaimed, holding her cupped hand two inches from her own eye socket.

"They're taking her to the hospital right now and praying she hasn't been blinded. Now you tell me *exactly* what happened!"

So Micky explained everything in detail yet again, while his mother interrupted repeatedly to ask him if he was sure of everything he said and how this or that had occurred. At last she seemed to believe him, but still she sent him upstairs to his room from where he could hear her calling his father at work on the telephone.

60.

Discomfort

Paul never spent a comfortable moment in a hospital. Not that one could blame him, of course; people often fall victim to worse maladies in hospitals than the ones they came in to have treated and, of course, not everyone leaves a hospital alive. Paul had always enjoyed excellent health, a broken collar bone suffered in a college intramural touch football game being the only reason since he was born that he'd ever had to go to a hospital for personal care, but like most folks he'd made his share of visits to family and friends who were sick or injured. When his son was lying in a coma after being hit by a car as a boy, Paul and Joan had barely left his side and his six days of unconsciousness seemed to last forever. The experience had a permanent effect on both parents and the memory of it came to the forefront of Paul's thoughts every time he had occasion to walk into a medical facility. Combined with this was the discomfort of the feelings of guilt he felt at consciously not wanting to be there, of wanting to be almost anywhere else, while showing genuine sympathy for whoever he had come to see, sympathy that felt like an act somehow, because of his desire to be somewhere else. This wouldn't have bothered another man, but Paul wasn't someone accustomed to feeling guilty.

Joan had picked Paul up at the airport and they had driven directly to the hospital while she filled him in with the details that had been learned since they had spoken that afternoon. A woman from Harvey's neighborhood, Dorothy Schenley, Mrs. Ralph

Schenley, had gone to the police and reported that Harvey had come around the bend on the wrong side of the road and they had both swerved to avoid a head-on collision. She had then proceeded around the bend and kept going and was ignorant of the fact that Harvey had suffered a rollover until hours later when she returned home and, seeing the story of the FBI agent on the TV news, began to put two and two together. Mrs. Schenley told the police that things had happened so quickly that she couldn't be absolutely certain, but it had looked to her like a golden retriever had been trying to climb out the driver's window and she thought maybe the driver had strayed to the wrong side of the road as it curved to the right because he had been struggling with the animal and that it had perhaps obscured his view. The police had thanked her for coming forward and sent her home.

The first police to arrive at the overturned wreck had found Rufrak so unharmed that it didn't even occur to them he'd been a part of the accident. They reported that he had both seemed to be trying to "attend to" the injured man, who had hung suspended by his seatbelt, licking his face and such, and barked at those who had come running or stopped their cars at the scene, keeping the strangers at bay until the cops arrived, at which he appeared to recognize their authority and had actually welcomed them, then lain nearby and watched with concern while another cruiser, the ambulance and a fire truck came screaming up and the rescue was effected.

When Joan told her husband that pads on three of the dog's feet were scraped and bleeding, he guessed that Rufrak had actually jumped from the vehicle before it rolled.

Harvey had not been so lucky. He'd barely bled as much as the dog, but the big SUV had rolled two and a half times before coming to rest on its roof against a huge sycamore tree and he'd suffered a collapsed left lung, four broken ribs, fractured his left wrist and broken two vertebrae in his neck. When Paul and Joan entered his room they barely got a glance at him before his wife, who had been sitting at his bedside holding his hand, stood up and shuffled them back into the hall. Statuesque, raven-haired Janice Turner was famous for being the most unflappable, good-natured problem solver among all the wives in their circle of friends. Tonight was the first time the Warrens had ever seen her when she'd obviously been crying.

"Have you eaten?" Janice asked Paul.

"How is he?" asked Paul.

"Come on. Let's go to the cafeteria," Janice said and began to lead the way. "I need to eat something. Have you eaten, Paul?"

"I had some nuts and crackers on the plane," replied Paul, feeling both relief and guilt at the thought that at least in the cafeteria maybe he could pretend he was somewhere else, provided it didn't smell too strongly of disinfectant.

61.

Fear and Desire

Shortly after the Warrens arrived home from the hospital Frank Rhodes called. His inquiry at The Salvation Army Church had led to the information that there had been a burial at their cemetery on the day Sandra Callahan and Steven Beck had been reported missing. The head administrator, Thomas Emerson, had taken over after Minister Johan Beck had passed away, so this was all before his arrival, but as luck would have it, there was a man who had been a volunteer with the church at the time, a Fred Hughes, who had taken over Steven Beck's job and remembered a lot of details. These included the fact that there had been a heavy rain the night before and the morning of the burial and Hughes had to more or less re-dig the grave that Steven Beck had prepared the previous day, because the rain had practically collapsed its walls.

It being Saturday, there was nothing more that could be done during the remainder of the weekend, but Rhodes had already called both the family of the interred and a judge who was a close friend and had set things in motion to open the grave on Monday morning.

Further checking of the church records had shown that other burials had taken place on days that followed each of the other six disappearances. If they found what they expected to in the first grave, the others would also be opened.

None of this came as a surprise to Paul. He was certain that the rain explained why Beck's and Sandra's bodies had not been found in the bottom of the grave on the day of the burial and he was confident that the other women would also be uncovered beneath the caskets that belonged in each of the other concerned graves.

It had been a long day and Paul was exhausted, but after he and Joan retired for the night and made love with a passion that reflected both Paul's having been away and Harvey's accident having brought to the forefront the undeniable awareness that there's a thin line between life and death, a line that can suddenly be crossed and separate one from a loved one at any moment without any warning, he found he couldn't turn off his thoughts and sleep. He tossed and turned for nearly an hour before he finally got out of bed and went downstairs, first to the kitchen for a glass of milk – he poured a few ounces into Rufrak's bowl in the pantry where the dog had been lying, except for a brief visit to the yard, licking his wounded paws since Joan had brought him home that afternoon, doing so mainly to distract the animal from his licking – and then to the study where he clicked on the TV and sat in his recliner not watching it.

The broadcast was of an infomercial. A man named Brad Shields was telling his live studio audience members, who focused on him with rapt attention, that it's always a good time to take advantage of opportunities.

"And in a down market," insisted Shields, "with interest rates and home prices at a twenty-plus-year low, your opportunity to get in on great deals *now* is perhaps better than ever! It's all a matter of coming to grips with your fear and desire; your *fear* of what might happen in the future and your *desire* to become wealthy. So…"

The words fear and desire had caught Paul's ear. He listened to Shields for a few moments and then used the remote to turn off the television. He was thinking that Shields was probably a very successful salesman, because he was actually a motivational speaker.

Paul knew from experience that two of the primary motivators of human behavior were the desire to succeed and fear of failure. People highly motivated by the desire to succeed were most likely to succeed, while those motivated by fear of failure were more likely to avoid trying to do anything at which they might fail and thus never give success a chance.

Paul knew that, as a rule, serial predators saw themselves as failures, failures who blamed others for their failure and who preyed on their victims as a way of telling themselves they could succeed, even if that success was only at complete control over the fate of another person, with no lasting reward.

But not Orion, thought Paul. No, he told himself, Orion is motivated by success; he sees these people as vermin, a phenomenon of our overcrowded modern society that needs to be dealt with mercilessly, like an exterminator deals with a nest of rats. Orion is a man who pats himself on the back after a successful kill, then moves forward with the other business of his, no doubt, very successful life.

Most serial predators also save some possession of their victims – jewelry, underwear, IDs – as a trophy or a memento, to help them remember and relive their conquests. Paul was sure this was not the case with Orion. He left his trophy kills for his audience, the authorities, to find and he had no need whatsoever to relive his conquests in order to feel like he wasn't a failure.

62.

Thin Lines

It was now 1:07 AM on Sunday morning and Paul had been sitting at the drawing table in his studio for close to an hour after measuring out a shot of vodka and a shot of Kahlua from the bottles he kept in the liquor cabinet in his study and pouring them into his milk and then, after downing half of the white Russian, carrying the drink through the exterior study door and across the dew covered lawn and into the room of the garage that always smelled of oil paints. Paul wasn't much of a drinker. His father had had a drinking problem that Paul had become aware of when he was in junior high school. It was one of the few things he hadn't admired about the man and he had determined at that early age that it was one thing he definitely did not intend to emulate. As he sat looking at his drawing, to which he had added only a dozen short thin lines of ink since entering the studio this morning, he recalled someone's saying: too late we learn that our fathers didn't have all the answers and by that time we've become our fathers. Who was it who had said that? He struggled to remember, but he was unable to and it bothered him because he felt like he should know, that he did know, but it just wasn't coming to him. It was like his unfinished drawing, he told himself. It was like the mystery of Orion. It was like the dream that he now was hoping to have again and now hoping to complete, because he had become convinced that it held information of which he needed to become conscious.

Paul had had a problem with insomnia once before. It was during the time of his final exams at the end of his senior year in college. He had overstudied for each of them and was overly tired and though he was certain that he knew all of the material relevant to each course, he lay in bed for hours unable to relax and sleep the night before each day of testing. He remembered how the snoring of his roommate, Jon Rimbaud, had made him envious and he had to chuckle now. Jon had been a math major, was a certified genius, had earned his master's degree during his sophomore year by proving several of what had previously only been theories of quantum physics and was well on his way to earning his doctorate while Paul lay awake in the dark. The last time Paul had called him on the phone at his job at Lawrence Livermore Labs, within five minutes of his hanging up Paul had received a call from someone at the National Security Agency inquiring what his conversation with Dr. Rimbaud had been about. Paul had told the man that he had called about a Notre Dame class reunion and that Dr. Rimbaud had told him that, regrettably, he would be far too busy to attend. He didn't ask if the caller knew that he was speaking to an FBI agent and would ever after wish that he had. He was thinking about this when he heard Joan's voice at the studio door.

"Are you coming back to bed, baby?" she asked.

He turned to see her standing naked in the doorway, grinning at him coyly. He smiled and gladly replied, "Uh-huh."

63.

Confirmation

On Monday afternoon the call came from Captain Rhodes confirming that the bodies of Sandra Callahan and Steven Beck were indeed found approximately eight feet deep in the grave Steven had prepared the day before they were reported missing. Both were recovered with their intact driver's licenses, so the identifications were fairly certain. He told Paul that the coroner was not optimistic about determining the cause of death in either case, but of course it was too soon to tell what the forensic examinations might eventually find. Arrangements had been made to open six more graves beginning Tuesday morning.

"As for Washburn," said Rhodes, "he confessed to processing his wife's body in the machine they used at his plant to make fish meal for fertilizer out of the scraps that can't be otherwise used. After all these years we're not likely to find any evidence of her, but we shouldn't need any. He wants to do penance."

"Penance, huh?"

"Yeah, that's what he said."

Paul spent several hours of the remainder of the afternoon on his computer searching for evidence that Orion had been active previous to the Beck murder and was unable to find any.

He spoke with Janice Turner about Harvey's condition, which was no better and no worse. On Saturday night he had been secretly relieved when she had told them that it really wouldn't be necessary for them to visit the hospital while Harvey was still unconscious. Joan, however, arrived there before noon on both Sunday and Monday and lunched with Janice in the hospital cafeteria. She intended to continue to do so.

Shortly after three o'clock a call came from the district attorney's office in St. Louis asking if Paul would be interested in being an expert witness for the prosecution in a multiple homicide case. Paul spoke with the D.A.'s secretary for a while, asked her when they were going to trial, then asked her to fax him a synopsis of the file. Like many people in his field, he had found that, in retirement, appearing in court as an expert witness for the prosecution, and very occasionally for the defense, could provide a lucrative supplement to his income. He and Joan had invested wisely over the years in commercial real estate and he had a good retirement plan, but the downturn the economy had taken in the last years of the George W. Bush administration was hurting nearly everyone and in pursuing Orion his travel expenses alone had amounted to a hefty sum, so he welcomed the opportunity to make up for the dollars that were coming out of his own pocket in this case.

Tuesday and Wednesday brought the news from Alaska that the remaining six graves held the bodies of the other missing Juneau women and Captain Rhodes said that forensics had discovered evidence that Steven Beck had used the cemetery's above ground holding crypt as a torture chamber and to store the dead women's bodies while awaiting the opportunity to bury them.

On Wednesday afternoon Paul spoke with the D.A. in St. Louis and arranged to come there the following week to study the file on their accused killer. It appeared that the prosecution's case was thoroughly solid and Paul agreed to work with him and testify at the trial, if everything continued to be copacetic.

Thursday, as Paul sat at the kitchen table eating a ham and cheese sandwich for lunch, while Rufrak eyed him enviously, a beautiful African American news anchorwoman on his television informed him that a patient named Daniel David O'Reilly at The Heggerty Institution For The Criminally Insane in Albany, New York, who had confessed to the 2005 serial killings of women found along Route 88 from Schenectady to Schoharie, had hanged himself during the night.

64.

That's That

Paul wasted no time in getting on the phone to Albany's district attorney, a Mr. Dimitri Santa Monica. Because he had spoken to him previously about the man who had confessed to the Route 88 killings and been treated with professional cordiality, he assumed Santa Monica would be candid about the circumstances surrounding Daniel David O'Reilly's death. He was fortunate to find Santa Monica in his office, the man remembered him immediately and he was entirely forthcoming, even when Paul voiced his concerns that perhaps the dead man had been the victim of foul play.

"You can put your mind at rest," said Santa Monica. "Certainly this type of individual is not well liked and we're all familiar with how guys like Dahmer and DeSalvo were murdered while in custody, but the surveillance at Heggerty is state of the art and nobody entered O'Reilly's cell from the time he received his last medications at 9:18 PM – and he's alive and well on camera at this point, by the way, and the orderly never enters the cell – and the time he's seen hanging from a section of his bed frame that he jammed between the walls and the ceiling in one corner of the room. He fashioned a noose out his pajama bottoms. This was just after 12:35 AM this morning."

"You sound as if you've viewed the surveillance," said Paul.

"That I have. I took a lot of heat over this man's handiwork, Mr. Warren. I'm not about to take any over his death. My wake-up call this morning came from the head man at Heggerty, Everett St. Germaine, before three o'clock, because he knew I'd want to know. I asked him to the send digital recordings from the hallway to my office. I was downtown before five o'clock and I watched every minute of them as my first order of business today. Believe me, O'Reilly hanged himself. No one else could have."

"No one looked in on him for over three hours, so obviously he wasn't on suicide watch."

"Never showed any inclination to harm himself, so no, he'd never been on suicide watch. Not since the mandatory one we have them all on for seventy-two hours after they're first admitted."

"Well, I guess that's that then," said Paul.

"Yes, that's that," agreed Santa Monica.

65.

Digital Video Analysis

"Hola?"

"Hey, Bobby."

"Painter! Que pasa?"

"I need you to analyze some digital video for me, but you have to find it first."

"Okay."

"I'm going to give you a couple of names of men in Albany, New York. One is the district attorney, a Dimitri Santa Monica. He had the footage emailed to him at his office by an Everett St. Germaine from The Heggerty Institution For The Criminally Insane this morning."

"Alright. I'm guessing you don't have email addresses."

"No, but I'm sure the main one for the D.A.'s office is a matter of public record and you can go from there."

"Sure. Shouldn't be hard. What am I looking for once I get the video?"

"Well, anything that indicates that it's been altered, stopped and started, anything that indicates that it's not authentic and continuous surveillance video. If you can get into Heggerty's system, analyze the original and compare the two, that would be best. If there are any differences, give them special attention."

"Sounds doable."

"Good. Let me know if anything at all looks less than kosher. Secondly, and this is going to take you some time, I want you to access the exterior surveillance of the facility, especially the building where this hallway footage comes from, the perimeter of the whole institution and the parking lot. You're looking for someone who comes and goes before and after the hallway footage and either doesn't go through security or, if he does, he's passing himself off as someone he is not. Maybe a delivery person."

"Ay!…"

"Just look for anyone who looks suspicious. I'm not sure you'll find anyone at all. Just look for him. I'm thinking he's going to be well hidden. Imagine a special forces type operator or a sniper who is aware of the cameras. You probably won't see him, even if he's there."

"Madre de Dios," Bobby mumbled. "You don't ask for much."

"It's okay, Bobby. I don't expect much. Just look. If you see anyone, I'll consider it a stroke of luck."

"Bueno. How soon you need this?"

"Let me know about the hallway as soon as you can and then take your time with the rest. I've been told the equipment is state of the art, but I don't know how clear the resolution is going to be and I understand that it's night time."

"Si. Well… is that all?"

"That's all. Just remember you're dealing with the law, of course, so…"

"This goes without saying, Paint. They won't know I'm there."

"And if you could forward the hallway video to me discreetly, both what was emailed and the original, that would be good."

"No problema. That it?"

"Yeah, Bobby. And thanks."

"Oh. Well… you're welcome, Painter. My pleasure, I'm sure."

"Talk to you later."

"Later, Paint."

66.

The Bola Whip

Micky Landis was having another one of his nights during which he wished he were the only person alive. He'd been sleeping a deep and dreamless sleep when someone in one of the apartments upstairs in the rear of the building where he lived in a basement apartment, also in the back of the building, had turned their stereo on and then slid open the glass door that let out onto their deck and now what sounded like four or five young people were out there above him, drinking, smoking cigarettes and talking louder than the horrible heavy metal rock music that blared from the stereo's speakers.

He was thinking: It's after midnight, damn it! Why is everyone so inconsiderate of the fact that some people are trying to sleep at this hour?

He had slammed the big sliding window behind his bed shut, making a noise that they had heard, no doubt, because he'd heard a couple of them laugh and heard someone say, "Jeez, it's Friday night!"

"Not everyone has Saturday off, you know, you sons of bitches!" he'd responded, knowing they couldn't hear him.

He lay there and began to brood about everyone else in the world and soon was once more thinking about his older sister Ginny and how much he hated her.

On the day that he had accidentally struck Wendy Cartwright in the eye, he had waited in his room for his father to come home from work, fearing that he'd be feeling the sting of the man's belt on his backside, even though it had been an accident. He'd sometimes wondered why only he among the four children was ever disciplined with the belt. His father had generally been very easy going. It was his mom who had been the disciplinarian, too much so in Micky's opinion, but on the occasions when his father had been forced to sit Micky down and have a talk with him about something he'd done, he would calmly talk with the boy and listen to what he had to say in response and then, if he felt it was necessary to make sure Micky fully understood and would remember that whatever he had done was the kind of thing that could not be tolerated, he would take off his belt, turn the boy around and whip him across the buttocks with it two or three times. Micky realized now that Timmy had been too young for such treatment back then, but even as Timmy aged he had never been subjected to a belting and the girls, Ginny and his younger sister, Lee, maybe because they were girls, had never felt the belt either.

As it turned out, when his father arrived, he had called Micky's name out from the foot of the stairs and told him to come down to the kitchen where Micky was once more made to explain what had happened with Wendy, while his parents asked questions, his mother repeatedly asking, "Are you sure?"

Meanwhile, Ginny had come home from playing baseball at the park – Ginny had been a "tomboy", had always played sports with the neighborhood boys and was much better at and far more interested in these games than Micky – and then, when his parents had seemed to have heard all they wished to for the time being, they had looked at Micky and each other sternly, Lee was summoned from the den, where she had been playing with Timmy, who she adored and who she brought to the kitchen with her, and the family had sat down to dinner.

Before they'd finished, the phone had rung and Micky's mother had answered it. Micky could tell from what she'd had to say that he and his parents would be going to the Cartwright home after dinner and he'd, no doubt, be made to tell his side of the story there, yet again, and this is exactly what had happened, after which Micky had been instructed by his mother to apologize to Wendy for his lack of care. He had done so.

Wendy, with a large bandage over her swollen eye, had refused to shake his hand, but her parents had seemed satisfied and Micky and his parents had returned home to where Ginny was minding the two younger children.

Micky had been relieved when his mother told him, "You go brush your teeth and go right up to bed and think about your sins." He'd been pretty sure that his father would not be climbing the stairs and that he would not feel the belt and in the morning he'd been glad to awaken and realize that it had turned out that way.

But it wasn't over yet.

Late the next morning, while he was playing in his back yard, Wendy's older brother, Jerry, and five of his friends were suddenly there in the back yard of the house on the next street, on the other side of the white picket fence that separated that yard from the Landis yard. One of them had been holding up a toy bola for Micky to see, two red rubber balls attached to lengthy, yellow, plastic cords with a red wooden handle. He'd held it up by the middle of the two cords and loudly asked, "Hey Micky! You know what this is? It's the bola whip. And when we catch you, this is what you're gonna get." Then, while the others stood back and watched and Micky stared in horror, the boy had taken it by the handle and proceeded to whip the aluminum pole which supported Micky's neighbors' clothesline frame.

Micky had run in the house, slammed the kitchen door and cowered behind it, watching the boys through its window panes, as they laughed and shouted and took turns whipping the pole.

Eventually Micky's mother had come into the kitchen, seen him at the door and, looking outside, had witnessed the older boys and what they were doing. She had opened the door, heard their threats and angrily pushed open the screen door and shouted, "Now you stop that right now!" The whipping stopped as the six boys all looked in her direction.

She had stepped out onto the back stoop, descended the stairs and strode across the yard.

"How dare you threaten this little boy that way?" she'd asked at a pitched volume, pointing back towards her kitchen door. "Jerry Cartwright! I'm surprised at you! Do you know that your parents, your sister and Micky and my husband and I all sat down last night and determined that what happened yesterday was an unfortunate accident?"

"He punched her in the eye!" one of the boys had shouted.

"Who are you?" Micky's mother had loudly asked the bold boy. "I don't know you! You're not from this neighborhood! What is your name?"

The stranger had looked at the ground, then at one and another of his friends.

"Now you listen to me," Micky's mother had continued. "You get out of that yard, the bunch of you, and you leave Micky alone! What happened yesterday was an accident. Jerry, you come over here."

Jerry had obeyed.

"Jerry, your parents and Micky's father and I are satisfied that what happened happened by accident. Micky was reaching for the door and, if anything, he was trying to prevent it from striking your little sister. And she herself agreed that that explanation makes more sense than her friend striking her for no reason."

Jerry had said nothing, had just stood there shuffling his feet and looking embarrassed at having to be scolded by a neighbor in front of his friends.

"Now, I know you're a good boy and that you love your sister," Micky's mother had said and at this Jerry reddened, "But I'm really very surprised at this behavior, Jerry."

The boys had all reluctantly retreated around the west end of the neighbors' attached garage, leaving Jerry to bear the brunt of whatever this woman had to say. Micky had seen a couple of them peek back around the garage's corner as his mother's tone calmed.

"Who was that fresh boy?"

"Who?"

"The one who shouted that Micky punched her?"

"Oh. That was Davey."

"Davey who?"

"I don't know. He's Kenny's friend."

"Kenny Tyler's friend."

"Mmm."

"I might have known. And what business of this is his?"

Jerry had said nothing.

"Hmmph. You boys should be playing ball and not looking for trouble over a situation that has been resolved. Now, you go on now. I don't want to have to call your mother; she's got enough to worry about."

Jerry hastened to join his friends.

"And I'd advise you stay away from that Davey, Jerry. He's not a nice boy."

Micky's mother had come back in the house and asked him if he knew who that boy Davey was, but he hadn't recognized him.

67.

The Devil

For days after being threatened by the boys with the bola, Micky had been afraid to leave his house, almost too afraid to go into the yard, but eventually the urge to go for a ride on the nice, red bicycle he had received on the previous Christmas got the better of him. It was his first bike with twenty-four inch wheels and it was his most prized possession. It had made him feel like a big boy and was much faster than his old bike with its twenty inch wheels. He'd taken it from the place where he'd liked to keep it leaning against his father's big wooden ladder in the garage, walked it up the driveway, mounted it and gone sailing down the hill and around the corner toward the grammar school and the playground.

He had found his sister Ginny and a group of neighborhood girls, including Kenny Tyler's sisters, Donna and Maureen, sitting around the big, roofed, wooden sandbox that had stood next to the basketball courts behind the school before it was torn down to make way for the tennis courts. He had rolled up, dismounted and parked the bike on its kickstand in the shade of the sandbox roof. He'd only been chatting with the girls for a few minutes, mainly in response to their questions about what had occurred with Wendy, when he'd looked toward the southern end of the school and who should he see coming around the corner of the building but five of the six boys who had threatened him days before? Jerry Cartwright was not among them. It appeared to him that they had seen him as well and they'd seemed to be coming fast. He had turned and run in the other direction. He'd run across the parking lot, up the hill at the northern end of the school grounds, across the street and all the way home. It was only when he looked down the driveway into the garage that he even realized he'd been so scared he had left his new bike behind.

Twenty minutes had passed as he hid in the back yard and peeked around the corner of the garage to see if the boys were coming, then he'd come out to the street, crossed it and when he'd come to the property on the corner, he'd crossed the yard and peered around its corner toward the school. Wendy's house was the third one from the corner and he'd thought that maybe the boys were there with Jerry, but he made the decision to take a chance run across the street, through the Byrd's yard and into the woods behind it, which extended to the school grounds, hoping that the boys had not gone there to smoke cigarettes. He'd known that they sometimes did that.

From the edge of the woods he'd been able to see that everything appeared to be as he had left it, except that the boys and his bike were nowhere to be seen. He'd run to the sandbox, scanning the playing fields and could see no sign of his bike.

"Where's my bike?" he'd inquired of Ginny. She'd been silent, but the other girls had laughed.

"Did they steal my bike?" he'd asked his sister.

"No," Maureen Tyler had answered and the other girls, excepting Ginny, had laughed some more.

He'd looked Maureen in the eye and asked, "Well, where is it then?"

Then, as the laughter grew louder, he had spied one of his handgrips protruding from the sand. He'd had a hard time pulling it up, but when he had it standing, he was able to see that the chain, gears and sprockets were caked with sand.

He had looked at Ginny and asked, "You let them do this and you couldn't even tell me where it was?" She'd just looked away and said something to the other girls who were continuing to laugh at him.

With some difficulty he had managed to roll his bike home, not even realizing he had walked right past the Cartwrights' house until he was almost to the corner of his street. He'd taken it to the back yard and carefully washed it clean, then inverted it and re-oiled the chain, gears, sprockets and front axle and made sure everything was turning smoothly without any gritty sound or feel. Then he'd stood it up on its kickstand and gone in the house. His anger towards his sister hadn't dissipated any.

He'd gone to his room, found a ballpoint pen in his desk drawer, gone in his sisters' room and sat on Ginny's bed. Then he'd moved her pillow aside and, as skillfully as he could, he'd drawn a very good likeness of a snarling devil on the sheet directly below where her head would rest.

That night his father hadn't even bothered to sit him down for a little talk. He'd just come to Micky's room, where his mother had sent Micky after Ginny had found the drawing and gone hollering to her about it, he'd closed the door, removed his belt and used it on the boy.

68.

Ambient Light

"Well, as you can see, there is nothing to see, not in the third floor hallway video I sent you and there's nothing on any of the other video either, at least nothing you can see with the naked eye."

Backdoor Bobby had been up all night analyzing digital video footage and computer data from The Heggerty Institution. He called Paul just after nine in the morning and he sounded tired.

"But from ten to midnight everything from the cameras on the west side of the property, the west side of building four and its roof, and we can assume the video from the stairway from the roof to the third floor and the hallway, is from another night."

"And you know this how?" asked Paul.

"Well, when I didn't see anything, I made the assumption that there had been a switch, which is actually easy to do by simply programming the system to copy old data that it already has, but with the desired time stamp instead of the one on the copied data. So I started analyzing exterior footage on the oscilloscope for variations in ambient light and it was obvious right away that the stuff from the western cameras, beginning at ten o'clock, was suddenly different."

"Different?"

"Si. The light is always changing, of course, but once you eliminate the artificial light data from the wave pattern, the natural light changes slowly throughout the course of the night or day, but in this case there's suddenly a whole new wave beginning at ten. Then at midnight it changes again and we can assume that's when it went back to real time."

"Okay, I follow you," said Paul. "This programming of the computer... can this be done from elsewhere or would you have to..."

"I could do it from here, Paint. You just need to know what to do. It would only require the know-how and a lot of analysis of the system. Then you decide what data you want to copy, write a program and upload it."

"Is there evidence of that in the system?"

"Well, there must be on the hard drive, of course, but you write the program to erase itself when it's done what you want it to do, so..."

"Okay, I know what you're saying."

"But it's gotta be there on the hard drive, if you want to find it."

"No... I think I know what I need to know just in knowing that there was a substitution."

"The substitute data is very similar, Paint. I found when it's from."

"Yeah?"

"Yeah, it's identical to the data from exactly one month earlier."

"When there was no moon."

"Si."

"Okay, Bobby," Paul said and Bobby was hoping he'd be able to get some sleep now.

"That it, man? I really need to crash."

"One more thing. How much of an expert would somebody have to be to write this program?"

"Well, he wouldn't need to be a genius, Paint, just someone who's done his homework. You could learn to do it yourself in a few weeks, if you put your mind to it. Of course you could hire someone to do it for you, too."

"Okay, Bobby. Thanks for the speed on this. Get some shut-eye."

"No problema, jefe. I'm halfway there."

As he hung up, Paul was thinking he wouldn't need to be a genius, but in this instance he just might be one. Breaking into Heggerty, killing Daniel David O'Reilly and getting back out again undetected took far more skill than what was required to simply reprogram the surveillance system and he was certain that this is exactly what had happened. He had compared the pictures from the Jerome Anthony Anthony hanging in Santa Rosa with those that he now had from O'Reilly's cell. The knots used in both nooses were absolutely identical. Orion had probably incapacitated both men with some sort of choke hold before he hung them, though it was evident from the scratches on their necks that they'd been conscious while hanging and had struggled to free themselves. Orion knew, no doubt, that it was rare for anyone who hung himself to break his neck.

69.

Sympathy and Empathy

On the plane to Saint Louis, Paul was thinking about the man he was preparing to testify against when it occurred to him that he hadn't done the one thing in regard to his assessment of Orion that had made him a pre-eminent profiler. He hadn't made any attempt to empathize with him.

In figuring out who a killer might be, it was necessary to get into his head. Knowing the types of people who became serial killers, one actually had to try to sympathize with their thinking in order to learn who they might be, but Paul had always taught the agents who he'd trained that it was necessary to take it to the next level of understanding and to actually attempt to empathize with them, to imagine being them on an emotional level.

Not everyone could do it and for those who could, it inevitably had terrible and permanent effects that were not at all pleasant. It changed people. It was a high price to pay to do the job of bringing murderers to justice and, knowing this, Paul now thought that perhaps this was why he had avoided even thinking about doing it with Orion.

Paul had been a lawman. He had always been primarily motivated to serve the cause of justice for the society at large and he knew Orion's motive was succeeding at his chosen course of revenge. Paul knew inside, without having to think about it, that he didn't want to have to experience the thinking that excepted vigilantism and, perhaps more importantly, he knew he didn't want to imagine what it was like to feel that being a vigilante was not only correct, but actually necessary, however he also knew that if he was ever going to figure out just who was capable of doing what Orion was doing, he would probably eventually have to do both.

70.

Naivety

" 'Ho's are born, not made," insisted George Washington Washington to the man in the cell next to his, Alexander Michael Dunlop, who was soon to be tried in St. Louis for murdering six prostitutes. Dunlop had been arguing that every one of his victims, every woman for that matter, had a choice in how she behaved and that, regardless of circumstances, it was her choices that determined whether or not she would be a whore.

Washington was a pimp and a killer. He thought Dunlop was naïve and he told him so.

"Yo' naïve, man. I been livin' 'round 'ho's my whole life. I know what I'm talkin' about. Sho, 'ho's got choices, same as anyone else, but what you don' un'erstan' is that 'ho's will always make the choices that 'ho's do."

Dunlop *was* naïve. He believed that Washington was his friend because he shared his cigarettes with him and gave him advice, never suspecting for one moment that Washington might be a spy for the D.A., Cleveland Beauregard III, and that he'd soon be testifying against him in his trial.

"Well, some of them are offered better choices than others," Dunlop said, thinking of Diane Nicholson, a young woman he had met through Yahoo Personals, who had confessed to him that she had been a call girl, but had given it up when one of her clients, a lawyer who claimed to love her, gave her six thousand dollars so she could quit tricking and pursue her dream of becoming a writer of fiction. After an intense night of lovemaking, when Dunlop was two years clean and sober and they'd been together for five weeks, she had asked him if he'd marry her and he had gladly agreed to. Then, after another month, she had left him, gone back to being a call girl and broken his heart. He had started drinking again and before too long had started killing prostitutes.

"That's my point, mothafucka! You jus' don' get it. Ever'body got better choices," said Washington, shaking his head with a laugh. " 'Ho's jus' don' *make* the better choices. It ain't in the' nature to."

Julian Scuncwissel was Dunlop's defense attorney. He had taken the high profile case in an effort to make a reputation for himself and he was in way over his head. It seemed he was always making that kind of bad decision, like not changing his name before beginning to practice law. Everyone in the St. Louis legal community referred to him as Juli Skunk.

At the other end of the scale was Adam Carbone, the assistant D.A. who would be acting as prosecutor in the case. He was only thirty-one years old, but since graduating from Harvard Law he had impressed everyone in St. Louis with his legal prowess. He had a photographic memory, unparalleled organizational skills and was possessed of an unshakably calm manner, that he attributed to the twice daily practice of transcendental meditation, which allowed him to maintain a level tone even in the midst of the most bitter arguments. What's more, he was good looking in a boyish way and had an ever present sense of humor. It was said that it was impossible not to like him, even as he strove to put you or your client in prison. He was a master chess player and a champion at tennis. He ran ten miles every other night before his dinner. He was exactly ten pounds heavier than the day he graduated from high school and probably wouldn't have weighed that much had he not intentionally put fifteen pounds of muscle on his upper body by lifting weights while in college, muscle that he now maintained primarily via a regimen of push-ups and pull-ups. He could do a dozen handstand push-ups. His wife, Morgan, was delighted that he still made love to her like a hungry teenager and as often as when they were newlyweds. Very successful attorneys are often called sharks and those skilled enough to defeat them regularly are said to eat sharks for breakfast. Rumor had it that Adam Carbone actually did dine on shark in the morning and, as Morgan Carbone could tell you, the rumor was based on fact.

Carbone had never lost a case. Given the chance, he would make a fool of Juli Skunk in the courtroom and Juli would come away from the experience respecting, even admiring him for having done so.

Alexander Michael Dunlop sat on the edge of his cot thinking to himself: my mistake was that I loved somebody who didn't deserve my love.

71.

Personality

Ultimately, personality in inescapable. From the moment Paul met St. Louis District Attorney Cleveland Beauregard III he didn't like him. Beauregard tried to project the public image of a do-gooder and an unselfish servant of the people, but Paul detected something else in his personality.

During his cab ride from Lambert-St. Louis Airport to the D.A.'s office, Paul had observed campaign posters featuring Beauregard's beaming visage and the slogan "For The Future of Missouri", which informed him that the man was seeking the office of State Attorney General in the nearing election. His smile immediately struck Paul as being forced, completely insincere. It gave him a feeling of foreboding.

Some people are not at all motivated by the desire to be liked by others. The desire to be dominant in their own imaginations supplants all else. When Beauregard's secretary had shown Paul to the D.A.'s inner office, the man rose from behind his enormous mahogany desk, fastened the middle button of his light gray Armani suit coat around his considerable girth and, managing the same phony smile seen on his posters, circumnavigated his desk to grasp Paul's hand and shake it far too firmly and enthusiastically, saying, "Cleveland Beauregard The Third, Mr. Warren! So glad you could come to help us. How was your trip, sir?"

It was obvious to Paul that Beauregard didn't actually care. "It was just fine, thank-you," he replied.

Beauregard had an English bulldog that he insisted on bringing along to his office every day and Paul could tell by the way the dog reacted to Beauregard that he was a man who beat his wife. Like a serial murderer, he was motivated by the need to overcome his feelings of inadequacy. This is not at all uncommon in politicians and, in extreme cases, leads to people like Hitler or Saddam Hussein. On the other hand, people who are blessed with an awareness of their own powers of creativity and confidence in their own capabilities are perhaps the best examples of the type not prone to the destruction of others and, for this very reason, they often attract jealousy and animosity as well as admiration.

Immediately, Beauregard turned the conversation to the rigors of his campaign for higher office, insisting that he was, however, glad to do whatever it would take to win, because Missourians were depending upon his success, and he very quickly made it plain that he'd be handing Paul off to his assistant D.A., Adam Carbone, who momentarily arrived, was introduced and thankfully rescued Paul from Beauregard's presence.

Once outside of his boss's office, Carbone candidly remarked that Beauregard was counting on riding the publicity of the success of their prosecution of Alexander Michael Dunlop to win enough voter approval to become the next attorney general of the state.

"I see," said Paul.

Carbone examined Paul's eyes for just a moment before he felt he could say, "He's an idiot, you know."

72.

The Phenomenon

"Here's the thing," said Carbone to Paul when they were settled into the former's office and had been discussing the serial killer phenomenon for several minutes, "I've read a lot about these guys, Ressler's and Douglas's books mainly, and I've got a theory about why we see them primarily in certain countries, the U.S., England, Russia, Germany, South Africa. I think it's related to leisure."

"Leisure?"

"Yeah, leisure. Ressler says it's seen mainly in what he calls the 'more advanced' countries, right? But I think the common factor is more related to people living in societies where there are a lot of people who are free to explore personal pleasures, whatever that may entail, societies where survival and work isn't everything and people are not only allowed a great deal of privilege, but they feel they are entitled to it. And then there are some people who feel they aren't getting their fair share and, if they're warped enough, they strike back at the community by victimizing others in a society that is relaxed enough to give them the freedom to do so."

"Uh-huh. So how does this correspond to your boy, Dunlop?"

"Oh, Dunlop is a perfect example. To begin with, he's an American. We're the most privileged society on Earth and, as you well know, we've got more of these sick fucks than anywhere else. He got sober and came to feel he had a right to what they call in Alcoholics Anonymous 'a life second to none.' He meets a former hooker who he thinks he's better than to begin with, treats her very well, has great sex and after she proposes to him, he begins to make big plans for the future, including dumping a roommate, with whom he's lived since getting sober, and renting a bigger, better, more expensive apartment, not just for him and her remember, but for her baby by another man as well. Then, when she dumps him and goes back to being a call girl, he starts drinking again and immediately feels that he's not only missed out on this great future he's imagined, but he's now a drunk again in a living situation he can't afford, with two years of sobriety up in smoke, all so that she can be free to screw guys who can afford to pay her. So what does he do? He attacks prostitution! And what's more, he feels he has the right to because it stole from him."

"But he doesn't attack her."

"No, because he believes he still loves her, but there's evidence that he called the lawyer whose mistress she used to be, thinking maybe that she'd gone back to him and possibly thinking he might be able to blackmail him, because he believed he was married, but discovered he's not."

"Really?"

"Oh, yeah."

The phone on Carbone's desk buzzed. "Excuse me," he said and lifted the receiver.

"Yes? … Okay, put him on." Carbone covered the mouthpiece, looked at Paul and said, "It's Dunlop's lawyer." Paul nodded.

"Hello, Juli. What can I do for you?" Paul saw the smile vanish from Carbone's face. "Well he has that right of course, Juli, but may I ask why? … Oh. I see… Well," Carbone looked at his watch, "I'll see you in the morning then… G'bye."

Carbone placed the receiver in its cradle, looked at Paul, and shaking his head said, "He's seen the witness list and knows that the guy in the cell next to his client is in Beauregard's pocket and that he told him everything. He says Dunlop wants to change his plea to guilty now to avoid the death penalty." He rolled his eyes at the ceiling, ran his hands through his hair and exclaimed without raising his voice, "That fucking idiot! We didn't need a spy! I told him we had this guy dead to rights! We didn't need any more information at all and that moron has become so obsessed with winning his election that now…" Blowing out a breath, he shook his head. Then he sighed and looked at his watch again. "Well, what's done is done. You want to get a drink and a good steak?"

73.

Vermin

"It's bad enough that this bastard was going to get the benefit of the appeals process;" mused Carbone, as he and Paul rode an elevator down to the lobby of his office building, "now he's going to get off with life."

"Life in prison," said Paul.

"Yes, but life!" Carbone exclaimed. "And he doesn't deserve to live. These people are vermin, Paul, and they deserve to be exterminated like vermin."

Paul looked the younger man in the eye and tried to sound sympathetic, as he said, "Well, I know it's small consolation, but I'm quite sure you're not the only one who feels that way."

"Yeah, well…" answered Carbone as the elevator doors slid open and the men emerged into the lobby. "Sorry you had to come all this way for nothing. You'll get your full fee, of course."

"I appreciate that, Adam," Paul said. "And nothing's ever for nothing."

"That's the spirit. Gotta always maintain a positive philosophy in this line of work," said Carbone with a smile, as they stepped out onto the busy sidewalk. "And remember to eat well. You're gonna love this place. Best food in St. Louis. I hope you're hungry."

"I could eat a horse."

"They don't serve it," joked Carbone. "But they added buffalo to the menu recently. Have you ever had buffalo?"

"I love it! Beats beef by a mile," answered Paul.

"Centuries of outrunning Indians has bred that into them, no doubt."

"Oh, that's good. You're very quick."

74.

The Rage

Micky Landis was leaving Melton's Fashions that evening, having dropped off a bid for the shampooing of their carpets, when he spotted a gray haired man in his mid-fifties, sitting on a bench by the women's dressing rooms, holding his wife's purse in his lap.

A couple of weeks after the incident with Wendy Cartwright, Micky had accompanied his mother on a downtown shopping trip and she had left him to hold her purse by the dressing rooms in Cronin's Department Store while she tried on a dress. He always felt embarrassed when forced to do this and would try to keep the purse hidden by holding it firmly with both hands behind his back. On this day he had heard a loud crash, like someone had dropped a stack of dishes, and had looked off to his left to see if he could tell what had happened, when a voice came from his right saying, "Nice pocketbook, faggot," followed by a hard punch to his stomach. The punch had knocked the wind out of him and, as he'd gasped for air, he'd looked up to see Kenny Tyler and his friend Davey, who had delivered the blow, standing there grinning and laughing. In terror, he had scrambled into the hallway outside the curtained women's changing cubbyholes and begun bawling, as the older boys ran away.

Now, looking at this middle-aged man passively awaiting his wife's return, Micky's face and ears began to burn and he felt the rage begin to grow inside, as he remembered that long ago afternoon in Cronin's Department Store.

He had already spied his next target. A few weeks before, he had spotted her through the sliding glass door of a client's dining room, as she was hanging laundry to dry on her backyard clothesline. She had black hair, both piled on top of her head and hanging about her shoulders. Her hair had a white bow in it. She wore black toreador pants, a white sleeveless shirt and white, slip-on Keds sneakers with no socks. She appeared to him to be in her late twenties. Micky slid the door open a bit and could hear the song *Lollipop* on a radio which was propped in the woman's kitchen window, tuned to an oldies station.

She was chewing gum and singing along with The Chordettes, as she pinned clothing that looked to be hers alone to the line. He knew now that tonight he would be strangling and then sodomizing her.

75.

Orion's Obsession

Paul was able to arrange a flight home late in the afternoon after his lunch with Carbone and was happy to awaken the next morning in his own bed.

One thing Paul knew that Orion would have in common with other serial murderers was obsession and, as he raked the leaves around his home on what had turned out to be an unusually warm late October morning, he began to ponder just what Orion's obsession might be. Surely it was something more pointed than wiping out "the enemy", something deeply personal and rooted in Orion's childhood development. In all probability, eliminating enemies became linked to it during his military service. How many real enemies does a child have, after all? Paul thought it might be related to the perception, self perception and the perceptions of family and peers, of being better or worse than others. Could it be that Orion was obsessed with the need to see himself and be perceived by others as "the best" and that, once he had focused on serial murderers, he had set out to best both them and the authorities by eliminating them, like some perverse game?

Paul wondered what could have set him off on this course and for now it seemed his best answer was that something had probably happened that Orion had taken as a personal offense. What was it that Carbone had said about privilege? "They feel they are entitled to it. And then there are some people who feel they aren't getting their fair share." Perhaps Orion had felt entitled to the authorities' protection from serial murderers and some occurrence had caused him to feel that he wasn't getting that protection.

Paul recalled what his son had said when telling him about the philosophy of *A Course In Miracles*, that correct perception is knowledge. Of course this had made perfect sense to the detective. The task was determining which perceptions were correct. And when he had told Carbone that nothing is for nothing, he had meant it. Paul believed that everything that came into his purview contributed to his awareness.

Now Paul believed he knew what his dream had been pointing to. Tom McAdams had found himself in the unenviable position of having the justice system set free the man who everyone knew had murdered his daughter and had felt he had to take matters into his own hands. Paul thought that a similar thing might have occurred with Orion and, whatever his obsession was, it was now driving him to do what he was doing.

Paul spent the latter part of the morning cross-referencing data bases of people connected to victims of serial murder with various other criteria, including self employment, financial independence, law enforcement and military backgrounds, education and athletic and sport hunting histories, but all morning he felt like he was spinning his wheels, just doing busy work while he waited for the things in his mind to finish stewing, because he didn't really expect to find Orion among the data.

Sometimes a thing appears to be one thing and yet it is something else, something similar perhaps, but something else all the while. Orion was a serial killer, of course, but Paul understood that he was vastly different from every serial killer he'd ever dealt with or even heard of and he knew he'd have to focus on the dissimilarities in order to figure out who he was.

No act is truly random, but one thing that makes serial murderers hard to find is the randomness of who they chose to kill. Orion, on the other hand, only killed serial murderers. Serial killers feel compelled to kill and, while Orion may have felt compelled to take the course of action that he had, he did so moreover because he wanted to. He had made a clear decision to be an executioner or, as Adam Carbone had so clearly put it, an exterminator. What's more, he was good at it, very, very good at it, and this was a main reason why Paul didn't believe he'd turn up in his data bases. Paul was sure he wouldn't have a criminal record, so he didn't even include that factor in his searches, but he believed that Orion was a military trained killer, more than likely one with a special forces background and the problem with that was that any record of his true military history would most likely be non-existent.

When Joan arrived home from the hospital after lunch, she had some good news. She found Paul at his drawing table and related it to him. It seemed that Harvey might be coming out of his coma. He was by no means conscious, but at one point that morning by his bedside, Janice Turner had found something Joan had said funny and when she laughed out loud, Harvey had grunted. The women had looked at each other in surprise and then Janice had moved closer and purposely tried to laugh again in exactly the same way. Harvey had grunted again. They'd alerted the medical staff, who thought it was a very good sign. When Joan left the hospital, Harvey's doctor was counseling Janice on just what steps they might take next to help bring him around.

To say the least, Paul was relieved. He'd never said it, never really thought about it, but he couldn't help but know inside that his dog was at least partially responsible for what had happened to his former partner. He rose from his drawing table, held his wife in his arms and said, "Thank God."

Joan looked over his shoulder at his latest work and said, "You know I've never understood how in the world it is that you do this. I don't see anything there yet. I never do, the whole time you're drawing one of these, yet I know eventually it will turn out to be a perfect picture."

Paul turned and glanced down at his drawing, then looked at his wife and said, "Well, to begin with, I don't include one line that doesn't belong in the finished drawing."

76.

Trustworthiness

Tom McAdams had been one of Nevada's most successful real estate developers. During the latter half of the 1990s and the first years of the 21st century, he was the envy of every other developer in the Las Vegas area, as he led the charge in turning that city into one of the most booming areas of the country, when all over America nearly everyone who could manage to put a deal together was capitalizing on the fact that houses everywhere were appreciating. Nationwide, people had become aware that real estate was the key to financial freedom and some of the most aware were investing in Las Vegas, because houses there were appreciating at the rate of 30% per year. Tom had become a legend by attracting investors from all over the country and the world to Vegas with brilliant marketing strategies, beautiful properties, excellent prices, immediate friendly service, access to lenders and figures that showed the promise of quick profits. He'd made an awful lot of people wealthy.

What was not legendary about Tom, because it was classified information, was that in the early 1970s, during the Vietnam War, he had been part of the Phoenix Program, a secret assassination program. Even his wife, Shirley, was uninformed of his actual military history. She knew he had been a prisoner of war and had spent over two years in the Hanoi Hilton, the notorious North Vietnamese prison, but what she believed about how he had come to be captured before being sent there was not factual.

Tom liked to say, "Anyone who can't be trusted to hold your

safety line on a mountainside is not worthy to be called your friend." However, Tom wasn't a mountain climber in a literal sense. During the war his way of saying this same thing was, "Any man who isn't willing to lay down his life to save another's is not trustworthy enough to be on a mission with you."

On his last mission, near the Cambodian border, both he and his lieutenant had nearly been captured, but Tom had risked his own life and been severely wounded ensuring that the lieutenant escaped. The lieutenant would have made every effort to rescue Captain McAdams, in spite of his orders to bring back the intelligence they'd been after, but he himself had been so badly wounded that, had he been a weaker man, he'd have died long before he was able to signal for his eventual helicopter extraction from the jungle.

After Tom was taken into custody for killing his daughter's murderer in the hallway of the courthouse in Las Vegas, he once again found himself in a small cell and he remember how he had never been broken by his Vietnamese captors, despite the most unspeakable tortures to which they had subjected him, but now he knew that he was already partially broken, or he would never have done what he'd just done.

In the immediate aftermath of his killing of Andrew Travis Johansen, the news was flashed around the world and people everywhere, those who had been following Johansen's trial and those who had not, raised their voices in Tom's support. Emails, phone calls and telegrams flooded the courthouse, many insisting that he should not be charged with anything and that he should be set free immediately. Television and radio crews interviewed people in the streets and, almost without exception, anyone willing to voice his opinion suggested that Tom McAdams was a hero who had simply reacted emotionally but understandably in the wake of a failure of the justice system. Attorneys from all over the country were soon volunteering their services pro bono in his defense.

Of course he had been arrested and charged with murder. In the morning, at his arraignment, the famed defense attorney Benjamin Gallo entered a plea of not guilty on Tom's behalf and requested that, as a pillar of the community with an impeccable reputation and tremendous financial interests in the Las Vegas area, he be freed on his own recognizance, as he was certainly not a flight risk. Judge Harrison Stokes looked Assistant District Attorney Mary Offenburg straight in the eye and when she offered no argument, he ordered Tom's release without bail. It was a good sign, but it would be the last one for a while. Mary Offenburg was by no means happy to have drawn the case, but Tom McAdams had willfully killed a man in full view of the entire world and she was going to fight to see that he was held responsible for it. The fact of the matter was that the law was on her side.

77.

The Balance

It was with great reluctance that Paul remembered what befell Tom McAdams. It had been a terrible time and ultimately had played a great part in Paul's decision to seek an early retirement from the Bureau. As an FBI agent who had observed the killing of Andrew Travis Johansen at close range, he'd been placed near the top of the list of witnesses for the prosecution. He had come to know Tom over the previous months and, having seen the suffering of the man and his wife and having felt deep sympathy for them, he'd found that he was actually disinclined to blame him for what he had done. It had angered Paul that he would be compelled to testify against this man who had been so severely wronged by a deranged murderer and then had to watch as the case against that remorseless fiend was dismissed by the system he'd been depending upon for the only justice he could ever have hoped to see done.

In the ensuing months, Attorney Gallo had filed a series of motions for dismissal of the case on various grounds, all with no success. As the date of the trial approached, he came to believe that Tom McAdams's mental state, which psychiatric experts for both the defense and the prosecution agreed was deteriorating, would in the long run serve as his best defense.

Phillip and Andrea Smithson had meanwhile stayed as close to their best friends as ever. Andrea spent nearly as much time with them as she did in her own home. Phil Smithson, never one to sit still and ever the innovator, had opened a mainstream news division of his Gaming Broadcast Corporation and made it clear to all that his station would be setting the standard for truth and decency in regard to the case. He'd all but threatened the entire fourth estate that he would tolerate no sensationalizing or otherwise besmirching of the images of Tom McAdams or his family, implying that he would publicly shame anyone and everyone who dared do what his broadcasts would not.

GBCNews found that it had an overnight hit on its hands with its nightly editorial show, *What's Wrong With This Picture?*, which had premiered with a program on the serial murderer phenomenon and thereafter, whatever the focus of the show was, be it aspects of bad government, faulty manufacturing, drugs, gangs, the dreadful state of American public education or the overcrowded and ineffective penal systems, had broadcast a segment every night featuring another American serial killer. Privately, Smithson wished he had thought to create GBCNews and the show when Andrew Travis Johansen had first been arrested, but he now was determined to at least turn as much public sentiment as possible against these animals, while his friend's fate hung in the balance.

Finally, just days before the trial was set to begin, a deal had been struck. Tom McAdams had become so much a shell of his former self that the prosecution had serious doubts about his ability to stand trial and when Benjamin Gallo filed a motion to dismiss the case based on his diminished capacity and the prosecution's psychiatrists were evenly divided in their opinions, Mary Offenburg suggested that if Tom would plead guilty to manslaughter with special circumstances and accept confinement to a psychiatric institution until he was determined to be mentally healthy again, she would accept it.

Gallo had advised his client to take the deal. Shirley McAdams did so as well. Tom had agreed.

After only a few weeks of confinement, the nightmares of Tom's hellish days and nights in the Hanoi Hilton had begun. He was soon waking up screaming every night. His doctor had urged him to share his memories of Vietnam with him, to exercise regularly and begin a program of meditation twice a day. He'd increased Tom's medication levels. This had seemed to help for a while and then, as Tom had developed a tolerance for the drugs, things had become worse than ever. He'd lost his appetite and begun to grow thinner. The nightmares had followed him into his days. When his wife would visit, she could barely recognize him as being the man who had shared her bed only months before. She'd asked him how he was doing and he'd looked at her with hollow eyes and said, "How do I look?" She'd cried all the way home, where she'd begun to drink alone.

Then one morning, another patient, who would later explain that Tom had been ruining his sleep for weeks, had attacked him. They were being escorted down the hall in opposite directions and, as they passed each other, the man had whirled around and jammed a long pencil, which he had stolen from his doctor, in Tom's right ear. Tom had died within the hour.

Paul had attended the funeral along with what appeared to have been half the state of Nevada. The governor had been there. Paul had looked at Shirley McAdams, with Phillip and Andrea Smithson sitting on either side of her and, at her father's side, their daughter Veronica, who had been best friends with the murdered Heidi Anne McAdams, and he couldn't have helped but think that the newly widowed woman looked deader than her husband, lying there in his open casket.

78.

Habit

Another one had gotten away with it. His name was Alexander Michael Dunlop. He had murdered six women and now they were sentencing him to life in prison. As he read about him on the GBCNews homepage, Orion was disgusted with how they were letting him win, but he calmed himself and simply put him on the list in his mind. "Later," he said to himself. "I'll get you later."

He'd been following another story closely and now it seemed there'd been a new development in it. In the past twenty eight months, seven women between the ages of twenty-two and twenty-nine, all single, slender, dark haired and attractive, had vanished from an area north of Baton Rouge, Louisiana. Now there was an eighth. The most recent article had been picked up from the UPI News Service, was written by a Baton Rouge crime journalist and was quite detailed.

The latest missing woman was named Betty Reznick. She worked in a small record shop in Zachary, that sold mostly DVDs and CDs these days, but maintained a huge collection of old vinyl albums and singles. She lived alone in the first floor apartment of a duplex in a nice residential neighborhood of mostly single family homes. On election day, at 8:30 PM, she had spoken on the phone to her sister, Eileen, after returning home from voting for Barack Obama for president. She had been bright and cheerful, had told her sister that she thought Obama would be elected and that she believed it would mean a turnaround in how badly things had been going in

America since September 11th of 2001. She said she was going to put a stack of old 45RPM records on an ancient portable record player she loved to use because it reminded her of what she believed had been better times, the 1950s and 1960s, long before she was born, bake a big batch of oatmeal cookies, then sit and watch a DVD of Elvis Presley in *Blue Hawaii*, while using the cookies as scoops to eat a bowl of fudge ripple ice cream, before going to bed. Her sister had laughed, told her she'd never change and asked her how in the world she managed to never gain an ounce, before saying goodnight and hanging up.

In the morning, when Betty failed to show up for work, her boss had thought it strange, because she was always early and had never failed to call on the rare occasions when she'd not been well enough to come in. When he'd called her house and gotten no answer, he'd waited a while, tried again and then called Eileen. Eileen had called Betty's landlady, who had not seen Betty since the previous afternoon, but said she'd go and knock on her door. When the landlady called back and said she had let herself inside Betty's apartment and found nothing out of order except an unmade bed and no sign of Betty, Eileen then called the police.

The police had given her the typical response that Betty could not be considered missing until she hadn't been heard from for twenty-four hours, until Eileen was nearly ready to scream about her sister having been expected at work, that she had not arrived or called and that she was as neat as a pin and would never have willingly left her bed unmade.

She'd asked them if they didn't realize that several other women had disappeared from the area over the past couple of years. When the police told her again that she could come down to the station and file a report, she'd hung up, taken her three-year-old daughter in her arms, dashed out to her garage and hurriedly driven her Scion XD the two and a half miles to Betty's apartment, where she'd found exactly what the landlady had found and one thing more. In the middle of the kitchen table, stacked on a plate and covered in plastic wrap, was an arrangement of oatmeal cookies. There were two large circles of them on the bottom with one cookie missing, topped by two smaller circles and a final single cookie on top. The plastic wrap was loose around the plate where the one missing cookie had been. Eileen knew her sister well. Betty was a creature of habit with a compulsion for symmetry. She would never have taken the cookie that was missing from the bottom circles, but would have taken the single top one and then tightly fastened the plastic wrap around the plate again. Eileen had been certain that someone else had helped himself to a missing cookie. She'd gone in search of the landlady, praying it had been she. The women swore she would never have done such a thing.

Finally, when nobody could say they had seen or spoken to Betty for twenty-four hours, the police had accepted that she was indeed missing and they'd initiated a search for her, first county-wide, then state-wide. She remained missing.

Orion picked up the telephone on his desk and entered a series of numbers. After a few moments he said, "Hey, Gary... I'm good; you?... Glad to hear it... Listen, y'know how you used to tell me about hunting wild boar back in Arkansas?... Yeah, well, I think I'm ready to give that a whirl... Well, no, not in Arkansas. I've done a little research and I want to give Southeast Louisiana a try."

79.

Dreaming

Paul was dreaming of standing in the hallway of the courthouse in Las Vegas, Nevada with Harvey Turner and Mrs. Thomas McAdams. Just as it had been on that swelteringly hot day years ago, the air conditioning wasn't working in the dream and Shirley McAdams, who had kept her husband on just this side of sanity since their daughter had been taken, looked like she might faint. Their best friends, Phillip Smithson and his wife, Andrea, were there now insisting she have a seat on a nearby bench. Where was Tom McAdams anyhow? Oh, yes, he had excused himself and gone to the restroom. Paul had assumed he needed to be alone for a moment to be sick.

Now there was a commotion in the mass of people behind him in the hall, reporters mostly. Apparently the paperwork had been completed and Andrew Travis Johansen was about to join them in the hallway. Paul was suddenly terrified and he knew he knew why and knew just as clearly that he wouldn't be able to do anything about the reason why, because somehow whatever it was had already happened. He began to turn toward the commotion and he felt like his body was made of ice. He felt frozen and as he struggled to move, he thought his body would shatter from the stress he was exerting on it. He tried to force himself to move and he completed his turn. There were fifty or sixty people in that part of the hall, reporters extending microphones and beginning to shout questions.

There were lights and TV cameras, and although the man was among those farthest away from him, Paul immediately focused on Tom McAdams. Tom's attention, like that of everyone around him, seemed to be riveted on Andrew Travis Johansen, and as he closed the distance between himself and his daughter's murderer, Paul was sure, from the look on his face, he needed to be stopped.

Paul took three steps toward Andrew Travis Johansen, then quickly glanced back at his partner to see if he had spotted Tom McAdams and saw Harvey attending to the seated Shirley McAdams along with Andrea Smithson and Adam Carbone, who was the only one of the four looking toward the commotion. Carbone looked Paul in the eye and began to say something. Paul was wondering what Carbone was doing there, as he strained to listen to what the man was saying, when a phone rang, the dream was gone and Paul opened his eyes and rolled over to answer the phone. It turned out to be a wrong number and Paul lay back on his pillow mentally cursing the caller, trying to fathom why Adam Carbone had appeared in the dream in Phillip Smithson's place and wishing he knew what Carbone had been trying to tell him.

80.

Politics and Power

Orion and Gary Knayler were on their way to the airport to fly to Louisiana in one of Knayler's planes on a bright and beautiful, hot, desert morning. They were in Knayler's vintage Willys Jeep, that he had completely restored from the ground up, and Knayler was driving. The two men saw eye to eye on most things of importance, but one habit of Knayler's that truly annoyed Orion was his listening to talk radio. He had the radio on now, as they rolled along the highway, and it was tuned to a call-in show.

"Well, I don't think that by ignoring politics, you should be thinking that you will not be directly affected by the continuing economic turbulence," said a caller to the show's host.

"You got that right!" responded Knayler, shouting over the response of the show's host.

A nerve had been touched. Orion reached over, switched off the radio, looked at his friend and said, "What's far more disturbing than what that guy just said is that, these days, even having tremendous awareness of politics only seems to give people the knowledge that they are powerless to do anything at all about getting screwed in all the ways in which they are perfectly aware that they *are* being screwed. They think they're blessed to live in a so-called democracy, but the vote only empowers them to vote for those who will do absolutely nothing to improve their situations and they know that taking up arms will only lead to imprisonment or death. Meanwhile, any group protest or dissent is regulated and then ignored. Unfortunately, knowledge is not power, Bird, though the propaganda spun by the politicians and repeated ad infinitum by the mass media does help to further disempower those who are already virtually powerless. Only power is power, Bird. Only power is power. And political awareness amounts to nothing without real power."

"Amounts to nothing, eh?"

"Fucking A right! Think about 9-11. We've talked about this before. We know what the FAA and air defense protocols called for on that day and for a long time beforehand and if nothing else is obvious, we know that protocol was not followed on 9-11 and that *that* could only have happened on orders from someone powerful enough to give the orders and be obeyed and then not be held accountable. We *know* this, a whole lot of other people know this and have known it for a long time and more people, including pilots, scientists, law enforcement, firemen, military and ex-military people, are becoming aware of it every day. And what are any of us, or all of us put together, able to do about it except talk about it, huh?"

"Fuckin' A," said Knayler.

"Power, Bird. Everything is about power."

81.

Baton Rouge

When Orion and Knayler had landed in Baton Rouge and were en route to the car rental office, they began to overhear conversations about the arrest of a suspect in the disappearances of women from the area in the past couple of years. Orion insisted they stop and sit down a moment, opened his iPhone, got on the internet and went to the homepage of The Advocate and WBRZ News, Louisiana. Sure enough, the first article on the page reported that the Louisiana State Police had taken one Michael Albert Landis into custody just after dawn and were questioning him regarding the disappearances of eight women. The article said that Landis was a twenty-seven-year-old carpet cleaner from Zachary with no police record and that his fingerprints had matched one found at the home of Betty Reznick, the most recent woman to have gone missing. It further stated that Landis was known to have recently cleaned the carpets in the home of one of Ms. Reznick's neighbors and that police were checking his work records to see if he had cleaned carpets in homes near those of the other missing women. Police stated that Landis was thus far being fairly co-operative, but had, as yet, not actually confessed.

"Well," said Orion, "I guess we'll just have some lunch, keep the appointment with our real estate salesman and fly home this afternoon."

"We could still do a little boar hunting, Sport," suggested Knayler.

"Yeah, but it seems pointless now. If I like this piece of land, I'll buy it and the trip won't have been a total waste of time, but there's no need for a recon mission now, so let's just enjoy a good meal, see if the acreage is worth the investment and call it a day."

"Fair enough," said Knayler. He could see the disappointment in his friend's eyes. "Hey, at least *someone* got the guy."

"Mmm. At least someone got him, but will they execute him, or will they allow him to win?" asked Orion, but his mind was already drifting to thoughts of Alexander Michael Dunlop.

82.

Thanksgiving

When Thanksgiving came, Paul and Joan were very happy that Jeff, Alvina and Kurt had flown to Virginia the day before and would be staying until Sunday morning. The four adults all shared a love of Thanksgiving that applied to no other holiday, because it lacked the commercial hype and concern with gifts that accompanied Christmas, but, moreover, because it was a day of sharing a wonderful feast with loved ones (Jeff's favorite food was turkey, while Paul believed the sweet potato must be the finest tasting vegetable in all the world) and a focus on gratitude. When Jeff was a child, his parents had always emphasized that Thanksgiving was a uniquely American holiday and that Americans were similarly unique in the good fortune they enjoyed in terms of wealth, affluence and freedom, but especially in terms of opportunity, and they stressed that when one was born into an environment that offered so much, it was easy to take it for granted, so Thanksgiving was a time to remember to be grateful for everything that life in America afforded one.

When they'd finished dessert, Alvina put Kurt down for a nap and then joined her mother-in-law in the kitchen loading the dishwasher, while Paul and Jeff lingered over second cups of coffee.

"I ate too much," said Paul, as he loosened his belt a notch.

"I *always* do at Thanksgiving. I could have done without a second slice of pie, but I couldn't decide between apple and cherry, so I had to have both!" laughed Jeff.

"Ah, you never put on a pound. Enjoy it while you're young. I used to eat like that, but now over-eating really makes me uncomfortable."

"So shall we take the traditional after-Thanksgiving-dinner stroll, then?" Jeff asked.

"It's a good day for it. Unusually warm fall we've had. Let's ask the girls if they'd like to join us when we've finished this coffee, hmm?"

When their coffee was gone, they carried their cups and saucers to the kitchen and first inquired of their wives whether they could be of any help and were told that all was done, then Jeff said that he and his father thought they might go out to walk off some of their dinner and asked if the ladies might like to come along. Alvina asked if they might wait until Kurt had slept a while longer, Joan offered to stay with him and Alvina said she'd prefer to take him along, so they agreed to wait a bit and then Paul asked Jeff to come out to his studio.

When they'd arrived in the studio, Jeff spied the work in progress on his father's drawing table and asked him, "How's that case coming along?"

"I'm having a recurring nightmare...," began Paul in response.

"I've heard."

Paul looked quizzically at his son, then said, "Of course. She would tell you about that. Well... the thing is I've been thinking that it's trying to tell me something that I can't put my finger on... and then the other night a man I've only met once, Adam Carbone, the assistant D.A. in St. Louis, who I was going to be working with last month until the man he was about to try changed his plea, he suddenly appears in the dream and tries to tell me something, but the phone rang and woke me up and he never got to say it, but I can't get the idea out of my mind that it was going to be something important."

"Damn. That sure sucks," exclaimed Jeff sympathetically. "Well it's your dream. Have you thought about what you'd have him say?"

Paul rolled his eyes. "*I'd* have him tell me who my killer is, but Carbone wouldn't know and I don't either, so…"

"How about the things he *did* say to you? Have you thought about that? Could it be something he said to you in St. Louis?"

"I've tried to recall everything he said. We had one meeting and then had lunch together. The thing that stands out is that he expressed the opinion that serial murderers are 'vermin' and that they should be exterminated like vermin."

"You don't think *he's* your killer do you?" asked Jeff.

"Oh no," Paul replied. His son raised his eyebrows in question and the elder man said, "I've checked out his travel schedule. Hasn't left the St. Louis area since he and his wife vacationed in Hawaii last winter."

"Maybe he was going to tell you that Johansen should be exterminated."

"Maybe." Paul was now looking down at the drawing, hundreds of little lines of ink. "Your mother told me you'll be moving that big sculpture from L.A. to Chicago next month."

"Yeah. Oprah wants to bring it closer to home."

"Would you have time to do me a favor while you're in Los Angeles?"

"Depends on what it is."

Paul looked at his son with a furled brow.

"Hey, that's the answer you taught me to always give to that question, Dad!" laughed Jeff and, indeed, his father had taught him to never commit to doing a favor until the person asking the favor divulged just what that favor might consist of. "But of course I'll make the time to do whatever it is."

"There's a place in Beverly Hills called The Museum Of Television and Film. I want you to see if you can find all the news footage from the hallway of the Las Vegas Courthouse when Johansen was killed, everything you can, and send it to me."

"Will they let me send it to you?"

"I've called them. Yes, they will."

Jeff knew better than to ask if his father had inquired about having the museum staff send the video footage to him. "Sure thing, Dad. I was going to make a weekend of it anyhow. Anything in particular I should be looking for?"

"No. Just try to send everything they have that was shot by anyone from every angle," Paul answered. "I think someone may have caught something that might jar my brain."

"I would think most of that footage might jar the brain. I mean you've had nightmares about it for years now."

"I'm sorry to have to ask, Jeff..."

"Oh, no. Not at all, Dad. I'll be fine. Really. My generation was reared on ultra-violent video. And I'm prepared for this. I know what happened. I won't be shocked."

"Still..."

"Hey, Dad... fuggettaboutit!" Jeff said, in his best imitation of a goodfella, laughed and patted his father on the back.

83.

Son Of A Bitch

On Monday morning Paul called Adam Carbone. His secretary asked who was calling, then put him on hold and he listened to Dolly Parton and Kenny Rogers singing the chorus to *Islands In The Stream* before Carbone picked up.

"Hey, Paul. How was your Thanksgiving?"

"Just great, Adam. My son and daughter-in-law and grandson were here from New Mexico. Couldn't have been better. And yours?"

"Excellent. Ate like a bear. We had a full house. My parents, Morgan's parents, her twin sister and her husband and their two kids. So… I suppose you're calling about Dunlop."

"Well, yes I am," said Paul. "And I know how you feel about him, Adam, so this may seem like a strange request, but is there any way you can use your influence to let it be known that he's got to be watched out for so that he doesn't meet with 'an accident' in prison?"

"Oh…" There was surprise in Carbone's voice. "You haven't heard then."

" 'Haven't heard'? Haven't heard what?" asked Paul, anticipating the worst.

"I thought you may have heard the news already, thought that's why you were calling. He was shot this morning during his transfer, but not before he wounded a deputy sheriff, who's now hanging by a thread. Made a grab for the man's gun. There was a struggle and the deputy got the worst of it. Then his partner dropped Dunlop before he got five feet."

"He's dead?"

"Unfortunately, no. He's in the hospital, under heavy guard by a bunch of guys who wish he was, but no. Had a collapsed lung from a through and through, but he's gonna be fine. Wish I could say the same about the deputy."

"Pretty bad, huh?"

"Caught it under the chin. Exited the top of his head above the right eye, which he lost. I hope he makes it, but frankly…," Carbone trailed off.

"Oh, man."

"Yeah. Young guy. Wife. Two little ones."

"I'm sorry, Adam."

"Yeah, well. These things always suck, don't they? How's your ex-partner by the way?"

"He's still comatose, but he's reacting to his wife's voice. They think he's going to come around. Thanks for asking."

"Hey, I'm glad to hear that. Really."

"So Dunlop's under heavy guard."

"Don't you worry about Dunlop, Paul. Nothing's gonna happen to him… unless the man he shot, God forbid, doesn't make it. And if that should happen, then he'll fry like he should have to begin with."

"Of course," said Paul.

"And justice will be served."

"Yes, of course."

"Hey, why the concern over Dunlop in the first place, Paul?"

"Oh. Well, this is going to sound silly, but… well… I had this bad dream the other night."

"About Dunlop?"

"Yeah, about Dunlop," lied Paul. "But it doesn't matter now, I guess."

"Don't worry about Dunlop, Paul. Just say a prayer for the deputy, huh?"

"Sure, Adam. I will."

"Okay. Well, gotta be in court in about fifteen, so…"

"Thanks, Adam. Be good."

"I always am. See you, Paul."

"See you," said Paul and he hung up wondering why he was concerned over the safety of a son of a bitch like Dunlop.

84.

Desire and Acceptance

"My shrink told me that I'm a narcissist," said Andy Everly to his audience at the Comedy Store. "I said, 'Thanks a lot Doc. Tell me something I don't already know.'"

Jeff Warren laughed along with most of those in the audience, though the greater percentage of them didn't really get the joke and his own thoughts had begun to drift back to an idea he'd had earlier in the day for a new sculpture.

Jeff, like many college students, had done his share of partying and the accompanying indulgence in drinking and drug use before meeting Andy years ago at a meeting of Alcoholics Anonymous, when they were still students at The University of New Mexico at Santa Fe. There they had become familiar with *The Serenity Prayer*: God grant me the serenity to accept the things I cannot change, the courage to change the things I can and the wisdom to know the difference.

Jeff had taken an interest in Buddhism while still in high school. Buddhist philosophy teaches that desire is the root of all suffering. One desires that things be different than they are or, conversely, that change will not occur and feels the pain of disappointment in either case. Buddhism maintains that happiness lies in acceptance, in learning to be content with what is as it is. Jeff had become reacquainted with a spiritual path via the teachings of AA. He'd latched onto a line he'd noticed in *The Little Red Book* of AA that read, "The more one follows a spiritual path, the more it reveals itself." After a couple of years of following his personal path, he'd ultimately found that *A Course In Miracles* best suited his desire for spiritual contentment.

A Course In Miracles, like Buddhism, teaches that "the world of appearances" is deceptive. It says that reality is as it was created, that change is an illusion and, therefore, the key to happiness is forgiveness of all that appears to occur. All day today, from the time he had first begun disassembling his sculpture at The Los Angeles County Museum of Art, through his sojourn on his father's errand to The Museum of Television and Film, which he had found had been renamed The Paley Center for Media, and finally through his collecting of Andy at his Hollywood apartment and their drive to The Comedy Store, Jeff had been thinking about how *A Course In Miracles* espouses that there is no time except "the eternal now." He imagined his new work as being a functioning clock standing six feet high and fabricated of his favored titanium. It would have no numbers. In place of each number would be the word NOW. Its title would be *Eternity*.

"I saw Uri Geller on TV last night," Andy was saying. "You know, the guy who likes to bend spoons with his mind? Reminded me of a coke dealer I used to know... except that guy could bend your mind with a spoon!"

Jeff had never heard this joke before. He tilted his head back and laughed and then thought of how he'd often thanked heaven that he had never liked cocaine, how he'd always been too naturally hyperactive to enjoy stimulants, so his drugs of choice had always been alcohol and marijuana.

"I saw on the news recently that The Museum of Modern Art in New York is planning to auction off some of their inventory in order to raise funds, including a urinal that they're hoping will bring in a million dollars. Please! A million dollars for a modern art urinal? I guess they don't think it'll be all that hard to find someone who loves modern art so much that he's willing to piss away a million dollars on it."

Jeff took a pen from his pocket and wrote the words "Octin Sports" on a cocktail napkin having thought this would be the font he would use for the NOWs on his clock. While still at The Paley Center he had sent his father all the TV files he'd requested. He wasn't quite sure why, but now he thought that when he got back to Andy's apartment, where he'd be spending the night, he'd email him about the clock and how he'd come to conceive of it.

"We all know that former President Bush isn't all that bright…"

"*That's* an understatement!" shouted a man in the audience, which brought considerable laughter.

"Yes, it is an understatement," agreed Andy. "But when compared to some of the other men who held the job, it's absolutely shameful what a dope he is. I read the other day that JFK's I.Q. was actually measured to be twice what Bush's is… and this was *after* Kennedy had been shot in the head!"

85.

Blood

After the video footage of The Las Vegas Courthouse hallway arrived, Paul spent several hours reviewing it and for the most part he saw that things had transpired much as he'd remembered them. However, one thing that surprised him was, though he had glanced back to see if Harvey had also noticed that Tom McAdams was approaching Andrew Travis Johansen, he had not immediately turned to see Harvey's reaction after McAdams had slashed Johansen's throat. He concluded that his memory of the event must have been altered by his repeatedly dreaming that he had done so, but the video showed that he had been among the first persons to wrestle Tom away from Johansen and pin him to the floor, that in fact he had been the one to disarm Tom of the broken paper towel dispenser handle and only after that had he looked to see the horrified reactions of Harvey, Shirley McAdams and the Smithsons and Harvey was hastening to assist in the struggle that was now nearly under control, while Shirley McAdams had fainted and Phillip and Andrea Smithson were holding her upright in her seat and attempting to create some breathing space around them by ordering the few others who were focused on her to step back and give her some air.

Paul had also never dreamed, though he remembered it clearly now, that when Tom McAdams was grabbed and jerked away from Johansen, Johansen's attorney, Hugh Twillen, who had bear-hugged Tom from behind, had impacted a glass display case, which was set into the wall behind him, and it had spider-webbed, but thankfully not fallen apart and caused anyone to be injured.

What were perhaps most difficult to have to be reminded of were the animal-like wails of Tom McAdams, from the moment he was first seized until they subsided into whimpers after he had ceased to resist and was lying face down on the dark red carpet of the hallway, barely audible beneath the screaming and shouting of almost everyone, some now hollering for an ambulance for Johansen, others urging care that Tom not be hurt and, of course, the news crews barking questions and directives as they jockeyed to get better shots of the aftermath of the madness that had erupted.

Tom McAdams was eventually lifted to his feet and, barely able or willing to stand, was carried away to a holding cell in the basement. A damp handkerchief had revived Shirley McAdams, but she wept and babbled until she finally cried out and attempted to stand as they carried her husband away, only to fall into a dead faint again. An angry looking Phillip Smithson's gaze was diverted from the removal of his best friend to the face of one of two arriving paramedics and he loudly insisted that the man call for another ambulance for Shirley. The paramedics lowered their gurney, its wheels standing in a pool of blood seeping into the carpet next to the dying Johansen, gave each other looks that said, "This guy is a lost cause," and then the one at whom Smithson had shouted radioed for a second paramedic team, before joining his partner in futilely administering to the mortally wounded man.

All the while, courthouse staff tried to hustle people from the scene, yelling, "Clear this hallway!", "Everyone proceed to the nearest exit!" and "This is an emergency; everyone out now!", at which the news crews objected repeatedly that they had a right to be there covering the story, but eventually they too were driven from the hallway with the not-too-gentle reminder that admittance to the courthouse was a privilege, not a right.

Now, in his den, having watched it all several times non-stop over the course of the afternoon, Paul found himself looking at his sweaty hands, as he wiped them together. Among the other things he had not recalled until now was just how much of Andrew Travis Johansen's blood they had been covered in that day.

86.

Injustice

Orion was drinking gin and tonic and glaring through his office window at the night sky and the lights of the city below it. He was furious. He could feel his ears burning.

Alexander Michael Dunlop had tried to escape while being transferred to prison three days ago. He'd shot a Missouri deputy sheriff in the attempt and Orion had seen on the news three hours earlier that the lawman had died this afternoon. He was thinking over and over: when were they going to learn that these animals are not worth the powder it would take to blow them to hell? It wasn't enough that this scumbag had murdered six women and admitted it? They had to give him the opportunity to kill a young deputy and leave his widow and two young kids without a husband and father? And they call it a justice system! Where's the justice in that? They'd execute the bastard now of course, but they should not have allowed him to get off with life in the first place simply because he'd pled guilty to six murders! Damn the insanity of that!

He looked at his watch, saw that it was nearly nine o'clock, turned to his desk and picked up a remote control from it. He flicked on the television, which was mounted on the wall opposite the desk, and tuned it to the GBCNews. Then he walked to his liquor cabinet, mixed a fresh drink, returned to his desk and sat down.

When the editorial show came on, he turned the volume up louder than it needed to be and listened while the station editor,

Wayne Bender, sternly lectured about Alexander Michael Dunlop, his crimes, the leniency of his life sentence, his escape attempt, the shooting of the deputy, his death, the deputy's widow and children and the tragic injustice of it all. Bender concluded by looking into the camera lens and sighing, then with evident disgust asking, "Now do I really have to ask what's wrong with this picture?"

Orion turned off the television, then swiveled his chair clockwise to sit and stare out the window again.

87.

Reflection

The night after he'd examined the courthouse video, Paul was having the dream again. He was standing in the hallway of the courthouse with Harvey Turner, Shirley McAdams, and Mr. and Mrs. Phillip Smithson. Just as it had been on that swelteringly hot day four years ago, the air conditioning wasn't working in the dream and Shirley looked like she might faint. Phillip and Andrea Smithson were now insisting that she have a seat on a nearby bench. Where was Tom McAdams? Oh, yes, he had excused himself and gone to the restroom. Paul had assumed he had gone there to be sick.

Now there was a commotion in the mass of people behind him in the hall, reporters mostly. Apparently the paperwork had been completed and Andrew Travis Johansen was about to join them in the hallway. Paul was suddenly terrified and he knew he knew why and knew just as clearly that he wouldn't be able to do anything about the reason why, because somehow whatever it was had already happened. He began to turn toward the commotion. He felt like he was frozen solid and as he struggled to move, he thought his body would shatter from the stress he was exerting on it. He forced himself to move.

As he completed his turn, out of the fifty or sixty people in that part of the hall, reporters extending microphones and beginning to shout questions amid the lights and TV cameras, and although the man was among those farthest away from him, Paul immediately focused on Tom McAdams. Tom's attention, like that of everyone around him, seemed to be riveted on Andrew Travis Johansen. Paul glanced back at Harvey and saw that he, along with the Smithsons, was focusing on Shirley McAdams. Still trying to move toward Johansen, Paul once again turned his attention on Tom McAdams. As Tom closed the distance between himself and his daughter's murderer, Paul was sure, from the look on his face, he needed to be stopped. Paul started to shout, knowing it wouldn't help and he saw McAdams lunge at Andrew Travis Johansen from behind. Tom's left hand grabbed Johansen's hair and his right hand, which held the broken off, plastic handle from a men's room paper towel dispenser, in an instant came over the man's right shoulder, the makeshift blade found the left side of the man's neck and he slashed his throat in one stroke.

Now everything seemed to be happening in slow motion. Paul saw the horror and amazement in those closest to the spray of blood from Andrew Travis Johansen's jugular veins. He saw that Hugh Twillen, Johansen's attorney, had thrown his arms around McAdams from behind, had his arms pinned to his sides and was pulling him backwards away from his wounded client. A court officer had slammed into Tom from his left side just as a reporter did the same from the front, sending them all towards the glass display case, which was set into the wall behind Twillen. Paul had just stepped past Johansen, now on his knees clutching his profusely bleeding throat, when he saw in the glass of the display case the reflection of Adam Carbone, who looked him straight in the eye and said, "He's so obsessed with winning…"

Paul's eyes popped open. He was looking at his bedroom ceiling now, but what he was seeing in his mind was Carbone's reflection clearly saying what he had just said in the dream and he knew that

Carbone was not referring to McAdams. He was sure that his own subconscious had just clarified for him what Orion's obsession was.

88.

Right and Wrong

"Fruit of the poison tree they call it," said Orion to Gary Knayler, who was at the controls of his blue and white DeHavilland Canada DHC-3 Otter seaplane, as they climbed into the crystal clear sky southwest of Lake Mead. The plane had been a gift from Orion three years earlier. "One can't help but be reminded of the tree of knowledge in The Garden of Eden and how the eating of its fruit is supposed to have given Adam and Eve the knowledge of right and wrong, for which they were banished from The Garden by God."

"Mmm-hmm," was Knayler's response as he scanned his instrument panel then gently began to bank to starboard.

"We consider the understanding of the difference between right and wrong to be the difference between sanity and insanity, which makes you wonder what kind of god would punish his children for becoming sane."

Knayler thought about that for a moment, then, as he leveled off, said, "It's also referred to as 'the loss of innocence', Sport, which I guess would mean innocence by reason of insanity."

Orion looked down through the window beside him at a tiny boat towing two waterskiers and pondered Knayler's words for a few moments before saying, "Yet there's so much insanity in the world and here we are, cast out from The Garden, left to sort out all of the rights and wrongs of the world."

Knayler said nothing.

"And, of course," said Orion, "left to deal with those who knowingly do what is obviously wrong, only to have our justice system let them go free by means of things like the insanity of fruit of the poison tree rulings."

89.

Warning

Paul couldn't really sleep the rest of the night after Carbone appeared in his dream, so he got out of bed before dawn, showered and went downstairs to his den where he began reviewing the courthouse videos looking for a shot that might allow him to see what he actually may have glimpsed reflected in the glass of the display case. When he found that the NBC footage revealed that a KLAS cameraman shooting Shirley McAdams had panned to catch Andrew Travis Johansen coming down the hall, he switched to the KLAS video and soon saw himself stepping into the frame.

He had, of course, watched this video twice the previous afternoon, but had not concentrated on it heavily because so much of the action was blocked by people in the hall when the cameraman was unable to get close enough to shoot an unobstructed view, but as he watched it now he saw that, as Tom McAdams got within reach of Johansen, his own reflection and the crowded hallway was visible in the case's glass and, as McAdams grabbed Johansen, the camera came into view for a moment before the bright light on it caused a glare that washed out the entire video momentarily. Then the cameraman must have stepped to his right, because Paul could now again see himself approaching the bleeding Johansen just before McAdams was pulled away from him and in the reflection he again saw himself and the crowd in the hall behind him, including Harvey, who had taken a step or two toward the action, and Phillip Smithson behind Harvey. Then Hugh Twillen managed to pull McAdams free, the court officer and reporter slammed into McAdams, Twillen impacted the glass of the case, it broke and there was no longer any reflection that could be seen clearly in it, before the picture became a chaotic mass of rapidly moving people, as the cameraman struggled to get a shot of Johansen on the floor and the display case was no longer visible at all.

When Paul watched the video again, he stopped it when the glare occurred, then he copied the following ten seconds and opened the copy in a video application he had first used at the Bureau, which allowed him to zoom in on the reflection. He advanced it a mouse click at a time. When he got to where he could see Harvey and Phillip Smithson, he saw that Smithson seemed to be reacting to Tom's attacking of Johansen and, unless Paul was mistaken, he appeared to be saying something. After several more viewings, Paul was quite sure that he knew just what Smithson was saying and now he knew that he had to have seen him saying it in the reflection of the display case when it had actually occurred, though he hadn't consciously realized it, yet his dream had been a warning and had been trying to tell him about it all these years.

Why is it, he asked himself, that so often when you finally become aware of a truth, it seems so obvious that you wonder why you hadn't realized it all along?

90.

Rendition

Paul had gone out to his studio by the time Joan awoke and came down to her kitchen with Rufrak, but not before he'd called Backdoor Bobby and asked him to run a thorough check on the past three and a half years of Phillip Smithson's travels. Knowing that would take a good deal of time, he'd poured himself a second cup of coffee and then strolled across his frozen back lawn to the garage. Rufrak found him at his drawing table while Joan was toasting an English muffin and adding cream and sugar to her coffee, but she soon followed in the dog's tracks and, when she arrived in the studio, was surprised to see that Paul's drawing had become a rendition of a sunset over a Southwest American desert.

"Amazing!" she exclaimed.

"Thank-you," Paul replied, adding a short straight line of ink to the sky's upper left corner.

"So, I take it you've solved your case."

Paul arose, kissed her on the cheek and, taking her hand, began leading her back to the door to the yard saying, "Come with me. There's something I need your expert opinion on." Then he led her outside.

"I got an email from Jessica last night," said Joan, as they crossed the lawn toward the house. Jessica was the woman Joan's father had married a year ago, eight years after her mother had died following a thirteen year long battle with cancer. Randall Cook and Jessica had been constant companions for over five years before marrying.

Her first husband had been an oilman and had left her a king's ransom when he had passed away, the year after Gina Cook's passing. Jessica was twenty-two years younger than Randall and he said she made him feel like a kid again. Since the day they were married, the two had been traveling all around the world like wealthy vagabonds.

"Oh?"

"They're in Hawaii and they're seriously considering buying a house in Maui; can you believe it? But she said they'll be joining us in Santa Fe for Christmas!"

"That's terrific, Joanie. It'll be great to see them," said Paul, as he opened the door from the yard to his den. He bid her to enter, followed her inside and closed the door. "Now sit down here, please." He indicated the chair at his desk. She sat down and he flicked the spacer bar of his computer's keyboard, bringing the screen to life. It was obvious to Joan that he had put the computer to sleep while waiting for her to awaken, as he said, "Now watch this and tell me what this man is saying, please." Then he entered the command for the video program to run and Joan watched several seconds of Phillip Smithson's reflection until the glass case was broken.

"Yes," she said without hesitation, then turned and looked up at him. "He's very clearly saying 'yes'."

Paul nodded.

"Was that Phillip Smithson?" Joan asked.

"Yes," he nodded again. "Yes, it was."

Yes. Yes it was.

91.

Phillip Smithson

Everyone knew who Phillip Smithson was. While double-majoring in business and mass-communication at USC he had been an outstanding baseball player, a star center fielder with a career batting average of .339, but what had made him a college sports legend was that he'd also been a stellar running back for the USC Trojans and there were those who'd said that without him Jim Plunkett would never have been awarded the Heisman Trophy in 1970, the reasoning being that Plunkett was a great quarterback, but it was three seasons of Smithson's running, receptions, yardage gains and touchdowns that made him look so good. Some even argued that Smithson should have been awarded the Heisman, but it wasn't to be. Of course he'd been a first round draft pick, but then he'd shocked everyone by enlisting in the Army upon graduation and shipping off to Vietnam.

He'd returned from Southeast Asia three and a half years later, recovering from leg wounds that would have made a sports career out of the question for a normal man, but Smithson had proved to be anything but normal. He'd rejected the prescribed therapy and driven himself like a man possessed with a painful regimen of grueling training that had resulted in his arrival at tryouts for The Boston Red Sox in 1975.

His first season with The Red Sox had been nothing short of amazing. He'd played right field impeccably and batted .313. Of course his father, U.S. Senator Bryant M. Smithson, was a Boston

Brahmin and, though his work had often made it impossible for him to be at Fenway Park for games – he'd been chairman of more congressional committees than you could count on one hand, after all – he'd had box seats on the first base line and when he could attend he'd appeared to be the very personification of pride, though for a politician he'd been oddly standoffish with the sports press and had generally responded to their requests for comments on his son's achievements, on the infrequent occasions when he could be momentarily approached, with brief statements like, "He's a winner!" or "He's unstoppable; isn't he?" The press didn't seem to mind though, because Phillip Smithson could always be counted on for commentary that was both eloquent and humorous, while remaining humble, even self-effacing, and ever-complimentary of the team.

During his second season he was hitting so consistently that the entire team was inspired and for a while they were in first place. Then, like Red Sox fans had seen happen so many times before, The Yankees had offered The Red Sox a small fortune and a pitcher with an astonishing knuckleball for his contract and The Sox, as they had so often previously, had accepted the offer. The sports press had said that Smithson had asked for more money in his second year with The Red Sox than any second season player in history and had received it, which was true. They also had claimed that this had resulted in jealousy among the other players, which, if it had been true, was nowhere in evidence.

In any event, The Sox had needed the pitching and apparently couldn't refuse the money, so what was to be done?

What was done was that Smithson had made it known that he didn't want to be a Yankee and then he'd accepted a better offer. NBC had offered him an unprecedented amount for a rookie sports commentator and he'd left Boston for New York after all, but with the last laugh.

Phillip Smithson took to television like a fish took to water and audiences had loved him. He'd written his own copy and if it hadn't been enough that his analyses were always insightful, right from the start his predictions had always seemed to be clairvoyant. Men had quoted him in sports bull sessions and women who couldn't have given a damn for sports previously had tuned in religiously because of his irresistible sex appeal and because he'd made them laugh. In the sports commentary arena NBC had begun to rival ABC, traditionally *the* sports network.

When the invitations to celebrity golf tournaments had arrived his chance to shine again as an athlete had accompanied them and he didn't disappoint. Who knew that he'd once been captain of his high school's golf team and that his game had improved to the point where he might have played professionally? One afternoon after a breathtaking putting duel at Pebble Beach, from which Smithson had emerged the victor, O.J. Simpson had quipped on camera that Smithson was a hustler. Smithson had replied, "Look who's talking."

Like Simpson, Smithson had been offered movie and TV roles, but unlike Simpson he had passed up anything comedic or buffoonish. After half a dozen on-screen appearances as himself (behind NBC's sports desk), a cop, a lawyer, an FBI agent, a congressman and a marine, CBS had approached him about playing the lead in a TV series about a private detective, but, while his agent was holding out for more money, Tom Selleck's agent had sealed the deal and Selleck had become Magnum P.I. It was just as well that he hadn't landed the show, because ABC had been about to make him an offer he couldn't have refused and he'd soon become their senior sports anchor.

It was during his second year at ABC that he'd created and begun producing and starring in his show *The Hunt*, a weekend documentary show about hunting game in the wild.

This same year he'd developed a serious interest in games of chance, more as a student than a gambler, but as a very serious student, and this was how he'd come to conceive of a television broadcasting company dedicated to shows about gambling, which would eventually become his Gaming Broadcast Corporation.

92.

Real Estate

They say it takes money to make money and, while this isn't exactly always true, certainly having a good deal of money generally makes it much easier to make quite a bit more.

Phillip Smithson was very well off by the time he'd created The Gaming Broadcast Corporation, which he'd based in Las Vegas, and the advertising dollars that it brought in had put millions more in his pocket from day one. By the time his father had passed away from heart disease in 1990, the fortune the senator left him was a drop in the bucket compared to what Phillip had made on his own.

He had certainly taken advantage of the mentoring by his best friend, Tom McAdams, investing wisely in real estate, both commercial and residential, from the day he bought his first home, during his first season with The Red Sox, in Dover, Massachusetts, where he had been raised. He had foreseen the turnaround in the single family home market of 2007 and was fortunate not to have had any of his money tied up in places that lost their value when that had occurred. Of course, he owned The GBC Building in Vegas and the small casinos that occupied its first floor commanded rents that covered the mortgage payments on the entire property.

A year after he'd opened the news division of GBC, in fact the month after McAdams was murdered, he'd turned over the day to day operations of GBC to his management wizard, Gil Steinman, making him CEO, which, all but in name, he really already had been. Smithson had retained the title of corporation president and kept his office in the southwest corner of the GBC Building's top floor, but was, from then on, rarely to be found there.

It was at about this same time that he'd received a visit from Wall Street kingpin Garrison Danforth Saint James who informed him that an organization he represented would be very interested in backing him, if he would agree to run for the governorship of Nevada. In almost the same breath he said that this, of course, would just be a steppingstone toward an eventual run for the White House. Saint James assured him that he was confident in his organization's ability to make this all happen for Smithson. Smithson, who was not unfamiliar with Saint James's reputation, had simply replied, "The Bilderberg Group." Saint James unruffled response was that he could not at this time disclose who the members of his organization were, but that Smithson would shortly be receiving an invitation to attend one of their rather exclusive conferences, that they sincerely hoped he would attend and that they further hoped he would have given their offer of political support enough consideration by that time that he would agree to accept the offer. At this Smithson had struggled to refrain from sneering as he coolly told Saint James, "As you well know, I was raised in the home of a very powerful United States senator and, if I learned nothing else from that experience, I did learn that I would rather be stuck dealing blackjack in one of the casinos downstairs for the rest of my life than have to spend a single hour as a slimy politician. You needn't invite me to any of your Bilderbergers' conferences, Mr. Saint James. I've recently become semi-retired and I'm looking forward to enjoying my time with my family in pursuit of a life of leisure."

From the day he made Steinman his CEO forward, to all appearances his main occupation had involved traveling around the nation buying land and hunting on it. He'd bought large tracts of forest land, some with lakes on them or rivers running through them, entire mountains, an occasional big ranch or farm, from Maine to California, the primary criterion for making a purchase being that it had impressed him as a good place to hunt. Of course, with the bottom having dropped out of the real estate market and it being difficult to earn a good return on land, as compared to income property, even in a healthy market, land had been relatively inexpensive and plentiful and by taking advantage of what was a bad situation for most people in the real estate market, he had eventually become one of the biggest landowners in the country.

His constant companion on both his shopping and hunting trips had been his friend Gary Knayler, who he'd met in Vietnam and who had served as his pilot and also taught him to fly. Smithson had built runways at nearly all of his places and erected hangers on most of them. Knayler was a helicopter pilot as well and also a first rate mechanic and supervised the maintenance of all of Smithson's aircraft that he didn't personally perform. His prized possession was a Sikorsky S-43 amphibious airplane that had once belonged to Howard Hughes. Knayler kept the S-43 at his flight school on Lake Meade and had restored it to perfection. He'd named it Mary Anne, after his wife, who had died of lupus in 1993, and he could often be found sleeping aboard the plane.

Naturally, Andrea Smithson had, on occasion, joined Phillip on a trip to one or another of his "camps". Andrea was, after all, a country girl at heart, no stranger to hunting and, like her husband, could shoot the eye out of gnat at fifty yards. Veronica Smithson, who, like her father, had chosen to major in mass-communication at USC, seemed to be taking after her parents in her appreciation of the great outdoors and loved getting away from the confines of Los Angeles when her schedule would allow it. Much to her parents' pride, she appeared to have inherited their skill with firearms as well, having shot her first deer at the tender age of seven. Mostly however, Smithson and Knayler would disappear on their own for days and sometimes weeks at a time, flying, buying, arranging the building of small airfields and camps, enjoying semi-retirement and hunting.

93.

History

When Paul reviewed the information that Backdoor Bobby supplied him regarding Smithson's travels over the previous three years, it was obvious that he very well could have been in a position to have killed everyone Paul suspected he had. The man had flown all over the country and not only on commercial flights. There were also records of flights by his personal aircraft, both planes and helicopters, which he kept at his own airfields nationwide, having been piloted by himself and his private pilot, Gary Knayler. Plus there was no telling how many flights may have taken place for which no flight plans had been filed.

In checking Smithson's military record, Paul was not surprised to find that it was classified. There didn't appear to be any way of finding out what he had been trained for or done in Vietnam, but the fact that his record was top secret was in itself an indication to Paul that Smithson may well have been an operative in the special forces.

GBC's show *What's Wrong With This Picture?* had always invited viewers to access their database on serial killers and when Paul did so he found that it rivaled the FBI's in size and detail. It was updated constantly and one could therefore presume that Smithson was too.

What was most telling of all, however, was what Paul learned after a series of phone calls to Smithson's former friends and school teachers. Eventually he was able to speak with an old woman named Charlene Conroy, who had been Smithson's history teacher at St. Francis Xavier High School in Concord, Massachusetts when he was in his junior year.

Mrs. Conroy remembered Smithson as a brilliant boy who always seemed to be more interested in games and competition than he was in his curriculum, but after Paul had inquired whether he had shown any particular interest in historic events or social phenomenon, she recalled an outstanding paper the boy had written about the Boston Strangler and other serial killers (though FBI profiler Robert Ressler had not yet coined the term). She remembered that Phillip had explained that he had, like most residents of the greater Boston area, been alarmed at the murders when they were taking place years earlier, but what he had said "fascinated" him was not just that one individual would murder so many strangers, but that after the Boston Strangler case there appeared to be the emergence of other "mass murderers" across the entire country, as if Albert DeSalvo's killings had engendered the idea in the minds of other deranged individuals to do something similar to what he had done. She also recalled that Phillip was the first person whom she'd ever heard question whether DeSalvo was in fact the real Boston Strangler.

"And I remember how I got a chill to think how all the years later one of these fiends would strike so close to him with that poor McAdams girl's murder. I remember imagining how that must have effected him, this thing he had seen developing as a child now so prevalent that his best friend's daughter was now a victim of it," she said.

"Yes, I can see what you mean," agreed Paul, knowing all too well that the effects had been far greater than he could tell her.

Mrs. Conroy said, "I always knew that Phillip would do well in life. He could have done anything, but all he ever seemed to really care about was games, learning new games and becoming very, very good at them. He had such a brilliant mind that school work was like an afterthought for him, but who'd have guessed he'd do *so* well?" Then Paul thanked her for her time and was about to hang up when she asked, "You're sure he's not in trouble, is he?" She had asked earlier, when Paul had first identified himself and asked about Smithson.

"Oh no, not at all. As I said, he's just been receiving some odd, anonymous communications from someone who seems to know an awful lot about his school days and we'd like to try to find out who that might be," Paul lied.

"Oh yes, of course. I suppose that *What's Wrong With This Picture?* show attracts all kinds of mail. So many crazy people out there these days."

"Indeed it does, Mrs. Conroy, and this is probably nothing to worry about, so please don't give it a second thought."

"He was always so well liked, though. And he seemed to like everyone. Unless you did something he felt was very wrong, of course. He was never one to let anyone get the best of him. One time on the soccer field a boy from Marion Prep, a big boy with a reputation for very rough play, fouled him repeatedly and didn't get called for it and finally they got into a shoving match and both got thrown out of the game. Well, Phillip actually went to the boy's home and blackened his eye!"

"Really?"

"Oh yes, and he was suspended from school! His father had to come here all the way from Washington. It was a terrible mess. I think the boy's parents threatened to file assault charges, but I believe Senator Smithson made a financial settlement."

"Ahh."

"But I assure you this isn't who you're looking for. This boy – I remember his name; it was Sheffield Vanowen; his father owned a plastics company; only child and spoiled rotten – his parents gave him a new Corvette as a graduation present and he got drunk at his graduation party and ran it into a tree at a hundred miles an hour. Killed himself and one of the co-captains of his soccer team. Terrible tragedy."

"Absolutely."

"Well you know how some kids are. They think they're indestructible and then suddenly it's too late to teach them otherwise."

"I know just what you mean, Mrs. Conroy."

"But Phillip wasn't one who needed a lot of discipline, you understand. Far from it. More the type to keep others in line. But he really did go too far that time, you know."

"Yes, of course. Obviously. Well, thank you again for your help and you have a pleasant day, Mrs. Conroy."

"Oh, I'll do my best. You too, Mr. Warren. Good-bye."

"Bye now," said Paul and hung up.

Charlene Conroy's words echoed in his mind. "He could have done anything." No doubt, thought Paul, just as he had, Smithson had probably been told that over and over again while growing up and now he'd come to believe that there was nobody who could stop him from doing anything he chose to do.

94.

Sharing

" I don't know if you can hear me or not, Harv, but they tell me that it could help to talk to you, so here I am. Sorry I didn't come to see you all this time, but... well, I know you know how I feel about hospitals. I know that's not a good excuse, but... well..."

Paul looked at his ex-partner and sighed. He'd been standing next to his bed for several minutes just trying to get used to the severe change in the man's appearance. Joan had suggested that he visit Harvey, now that he'd solved his case. Harvey's doctors thought that familiar voices might reach him and help him to regain consciousness. Janice had even recorded and played messages from all of the kids. They wanted to come in person, but everyone agreed it was better that they not see their father in his present condition.

Joan was surprised at how readily Paul had agreed, but she didn't know that he'd been wanting to tell Harvey what he'd learned.

"So where do I begin?" Paul looked out the window at the snow that had begun falling as he was arriving at the hospital. "Well, I'm not having that recurring dream anymore... and now I know why I was having it. Remember when... well you would remember when, if... I don't know if right now you can, but remember when I told you that if I saw what I was expecting to see in Ogdensburg, I might have a theory to share with you? Well, the theory was that there was a serial killer out there killing other serial killers and, as incredible as that might have seemed at the time, at this point I know who it is."

Paul turned to look at Harvey and wished with all his soul that he might have seen a reaction, but there was none.

"And I don't know if the dream was a warning... I don't remember ever seeing the key details in it that would have forewarned me... but, Harvey, Phillip Smithson, standing right behind you in the hallway of that courthouse, when he saw Tom McAdams kill Johansen, he couldn't help but react. He said 'yes'. I don't know if he said it out loud, but he said it and I saw him say it... in the reflection of that glass case just before Hugh Twillen backed into it and broke it."

Paul sat down next to Harvey's bed.

"I've seen it since on video. News camera footage. There's no doubt about it. And there's no doubt Smithson fits the profile I put together and could very easily have been at the scene of every killing. What's more, I believe he was in the special forces in Vietnam, maybe even the Phoenix Program, and I found out yesterday that his interest in serial killers is not something that developed out of Heidi Anne's death. He's had a fascination with the phenomenon since he was a boy." Paul looked at Harvey and paused like he would have had the man been conscious and he were waiting for this all to sink in before saying, "And he's obsessed with winning, Harv. Sounds like the man the whole country's come to know and love, huh?"

Paul stroked his chin and his glance wandered around the room, finally lighting on a framed watercolor of a mountain reflecting in a lake on the opposite wall.

"The thing is, Harv, he's the best I've ever seen. If there's any proof of his involvement, I haven't found it yet."

Paul thought about how much better an artist he was than this Morley, whose watercolor he was eyeing.

"Well, I can't tell you how much better I feel now that I've shared this with you, Harv." He stood up, put on his coat and was about to say good-bye and leave, when he had a thought. He looked at Harvey and said, "Hey, I have an idea! Do you think they'd let me bring Rufrak in here?"

He was about to go to the nurses' station and ask about this and was at the door to the hall when he realized the best course of action was probably to call Janice and, if she agreed, have her appeal to Harvey's doctors.

He looked back at Harvey, the man who had looked like a professional linebacker all the time Paul had known him and now weighed a hundred and fifty pounds at best. "Hey, buddy, we'll see you soon," he said and departed.

95.

Crossing The Line

What could there have been in the life of a man like Phillip Smithson, wondered Paul, that could have led him to crossing the line, to stepping outside of what society deemed acceptable, and becoming a serial murderer? Certainly he'd had a fascination with the phenomenon of serial killers since he was a child, but he surely didn't simply make up his mind that if they could do it, and perhaps infect each other with the idea of doing it, now it was just his time to take revenge on them by adopting the roles of judge, jury and executioner. Of course he was obsessed with winning and he may well be considering hunting serial killers a game, but the failure of the justice system in the case against Andrew Travis Johansen was not the thing that caused him to become a murderer and it was doubtful that he'd pursued the course he had because he felt the need to take up a more challenging sport. It was surely something beyond the deaths of Heidi Anne, the injustice of her killer's release and the tragic decline and murder of his best friend, though certainly these events were the catalyst that had ultimately triggered his decision to begin hunting serial murderers, as Steven Beck's killing, coming only weeks after the death of Tom McAdams, appeared to indicate.

Every serial killer believes he is above and beyond the rules of his society and in Paul's experience every one of them came to this belief as a result of some extraordinary (in their view) experience that they felt had pushed them into a position of uniqueness, into a place where they felt entirely alone and, more importantly, a place where they came to believe that they now had the right to make decisions based on their own rules. Usually this experience involved a betrayal or a breach of trust, something that was deeply and intimately related to their sense of self and Paul believed that there was something of this nature in Smithson's past that had left him badly scarred, left him poised and ready to become a serial murderer should circumstances prompt him to do so.

Paul spent hour after hour, day after day, reading everything he could find that had been written about the man, including every scrap of information Backdoor Bobby could find about his and his family's history, but nothing stood out that hinted at being "the factor".

Late in the afternoon of a bitingly cold December day, he carefully removed the tape that held the new pen and ink desert landscape to his drawing board, intending to place it in the portfolio that held the other landscapes he had drawn while solving cases, and he stopped and sat down at the drawing table and just stared at it, knowing it was finished, knowing he was right about Smithson, but knowing a piece of the puzzle was still missing.

He and Joan would be flying to New Mexico in the morning. Tomorrow would be Christmas Eve and he knew it was time to go back in the house and help her finish packing, so he got up and found two sheets of tracing paper in a drawer, placed the drawing between them, then slid it into a cellophane envelope. He put the envelope in his landscape portfolio and closed the drawer in which it lay, knowing that on Christmas day he'd be asking his father-in-law things that perhaps only a man with a background like Randall Cook's would be privileged to know about.

96.

Gravity

One thing that Paul and Joan saw completely eye to eye on was the notion of traveling light. Of course they kept enough clothing in Santa Fe that they could have gone there at any time without any luggage at all and since they'd done their Christmas shopping for their family members online and had the gifts sent to them, they were unburdened by these parcels on their flight, so they were able to avoid having to check any bags and were flying with carry-on luggage only.

Paul was glad that they had booked an early morning flight and, since they were going west, the change in time zones would mean that a good part of the day would remain once they'd arrived.

They had left Rufrak with Janice shortly after sun-up. She had spoken to Harvey's doctor about bringing the dog to the hospital and he'd agreed that it was well worth a try. She was obviously enthusiastic about the idea and had once more thanked Paul for thinking of it before asking that they express her wishes for a Merry Christmas to everyone in Santa Fe and bidding them to have fun, a good trip and a wonderful time.

Paul was thinking about the effect he was hoping Rufrak might have on Harvey, when the in-flight movie came on. It was a science-fiction/action picture titled *Gravity*. The book had been a best seller by the popular author Eugene French the previous year. It was about an evil genius, Adrian von Darkk, who was bent on world domination. He had figured out that gravity, being the most dominant force in the universe, could be harnessed and used as a weapon of mass destruction. After demonstrating his ability to use it, by lifting and toppling The Great Pyramid of Khufu in Egypt, he attempted to hold the world hostage to his will. The hero was Josh Hemmings, an American James Bond type, with a genius level I.Q. and a photographic memory, who had the uncanny ability to fashion common objects into extremely useful devises at just the right time. The movie was directed by Mark Inlet, one of Hollywood's most successful action filmmakers. Paul disliked Inlet's films immensely, because he consistently took liberties with the laws of physics in them, often thereby making the solutions to his conflicts implausible. Paul hadn't read French's book, but he thought that in this film, since the premise of the crisis involved the suspension of the laws of physics, perhaps Inlet might, for a change, find a solution in the strict adherence to those laws, but the idea was not enough to make him suffer through watching it and what annoyed Paul even more was that the airline had exercised the poor judgment to show a movie about the potential dangers of gravity on an airliner in the first place. He found some classical music to listen to, reduced the volume and told Joan that he'd try to get some sleep. As was his usual strategy, he'd stayed up quite late the night before so that he'd be tired enough to doze while flying and, as Adrian von Darkk collapsed the Eiffel Tower, she saw that Paul was sound asleep.

97.

Trauma

Everyone else had exchanged and opened their gifts and Paul was looking forward to speaking with his father-in-law after their Christmas dinner, so it was troubling to him that Randall Cook had not yet made an appearance to accompany the rest of the family, all now settled around the dining table.

"Where is Randall?" he asked Jessica. He could hear Chopin playing over speakers in an adjoining room, but there didn't seem to be another sound coming from anywhere else in the house.

"Oh don't you worry, Paul. He'll be here. You don't think he'd miss all of this, do you?" she asked, indicating the sumptuous feast set before them.

Paul looked to Joan, who simply shrugged, then handed him a big bowl of sweet potatoes, apparently thinking this would command his full attention for the moment. He scooped some onto his plate then passed it to Jeff, saying, "Now we're happy, 'ey?"

"You bet!" answered Jeff, who helped himself to a large portion, passed the bowl to Alvina, then sampled a mouthful of the vegetable and said, "Mmm-mm! So good. *So* good!"

Paul heard the hinge springs of the kitchen door behind him and assumed that his father-in-law was finally joining them, but when he turned to see who was placing the Christmas ham on the table, he was shocked to find that it was Phillip Smithson, who grinned and said, "Surprised? Well, you ain't seen nothin' yet."

Paul was suddenly afraid for all of them, but before he could think of a single thing to say or do to protect them from the man, Smithson held his arms out before him, palms up, and slowly raised them. The table began to rise. Paul and his family stared in disbelief.

When the table was two feet off the floor, Smithson turned his hands over and dropped them and the table fell to the floor with a loud crash, causing everyone to jolt back in their chairs. Jeff shouted, "Hey!" Alvina cried out, "Oh!" Jessica was speechless, but her complexion had turned a ghostly pale. Kurt began to howl.

"What the hell do you think you're doing?" hollered Paul, pushing back his chair, standing and taking a step toward Smithson.

Smithson dismissively indicated with his left hand that Paul should hold back. "Sit down, Warren. I could do the same with this whole house. Would you like to see that?"

Paul hesitated, trying to decide whether to risk advancing on a man who might have the power to lift the house into the air or to withdraw and let that man have control over them all. He looked into his wife's eyes. She was clearly terrified, but her look seemed to indicate that she expected him to do something to rescue them all from the situation. His grandson continued to wail and Chopin's Nocturne Opus 9, No. 2 played on.

"You can't come in here and terrorize my family, you son of a bitch!" growled Paul, as he grabbed a plate from the table, flung it at Smithson and lunged for him, hands outstretched, with the intention of grabbing him by the head and twisting him to the floor with total control over him, but Smithson deftly sidestepped to his left and swung his trailing right leg into Paul's shins, tripping him and sending him to the floor, where he rolled over and looked up to see Smithson raise his arms with a look of pure malevolence in his eyes.

The room began to shake and plaster dust fell from the ceiling. From everywhere around them came the sounds of groaning, screeching and scraping, as the little adobe house tore loose from its foundation. The women all began to scream.

Paul awoke with a start. He could see that *Gravity* was now over. Joan was reading a magazine next to him. She looked from it to Paul, saw the look in his eyes and inquired, "What?"

98.

"The Best Gift We Could Have Received"

Jeff was waiting for his parents among an expectant throng of people at the terminal where their flight had arrived. They spied his beaming face, with its customary winter beard, as they emerged through the double glass doors into the non-passenger waiting area, greeted him with hugs and kisses and Joan allowed him to take her hand luggage before leading them to where he'd parked. As he was opening the rear cargo door of his Land Rover, Paul's cell phone began to ring. He took it from his pocket and flipped it open.

"Hello?"

"Paul, it's Janice." She sounded excited.

"Hi, Janice."

"Paul, Harvey is awake!" she exclaimed. "My God, Paul! Rufrak whimpered when he saw him, then licked his hand and barked once and, I tell you, Harv moved his hand and frowned, then he opened his eyes and looked at his hand, then he looked at the dog, like he'd simply been taking a nap!"

"My heavens…"

"What?" asked Joan. Paul held up his left index finger and winked at her as Janice continued.

"I can never thank you enough for thinking of doing this, Paul. My God, this is the best gift we could have received this Christmas. It's like a miracle!"

"It is, Janice, and it's the best gift any of us could have hoped for. Here, you tell Joan."

Paul handed the phone to his wife and Janice repeated the news to her while they all climbed into the vehicle. Jeff looked inquisitively at his father, who told him what Janice had said.

"Amazing!" said Jeff, as he turned the ignition key. "What can I say, Dad? That was one brilliant idea."

"She wants to talk to you." Joan handed the phone back to Paul.

Janice was now crying, but through her tears she said, "Thank-you so much, Paul. You've saved our lives, you know. I don't know how much more…"

"Now Janice, don't you worry. The worst is over now and everything's going to be all right."

"Yes, I know. I'm just… I'm just overwhelmed."

"Is he speaking?"

"Oh, yes! He said 'Rufrak', then he looked at me and said 'Janice' and his voice was very raspy, so he asked for some water. He's wide awake, Paul. He seems weak and he's speaking slowly. He's having some difficulty remembering some words he wants to say, but Doctor Kinkead says that's to be expected."

"Of course."

"He said he was hungry, too!"

"I can imagine."

"But I know he'll want to talk to you, Paul. I'm heading home now to get the kids and I'll call you back later when we're all here."

"I'll look forward to it, Janice."

"Paul?"

"Yes?"

"God bless you, Paul."

"Thank-you, Janice. Merry Christmas and God bless us all."

99.

Bighorn Lake

When Phillip Smithson was growing up, Christmas time was as often miserable as not. The primary reason was that his mother, Rosemary, who suffered from scoliosis and was prone to letting her emotions get the better of her, had a tendency to overdo things in preparation for the holiday. She had the best intentions, of course, and could have delegated more of what needed to be done to others, their housekeepers or other assistants, but she loved shopping and would spend hours, too many hours, in search of every last little thing that she thought might make the day just a little more enjoyable for her family and she believed she had to supervise every detail of anything she felt needed doing at home, so by the time Christmas actually arrived, she was generally both exhausted and resentful that her husband and son had not knocked themselves out being helpful, yet it appeared to her that they were expectantly anticipating a perfect day. This often resulted in Rosemary Smithson's spending Christmas day in a sickbed sulking and being not at all hesitant to express her anger over how all her work had resulted in her inability to enjoy the day that everyone else was enjoying because she had made it possible.

Despite the facts that Smithson always made every effort for his family's Christmas seasons to be completely enjoyable and that they always were, he never exactly looked forward to Christmas, because he'd become accustomed to the dynamic of his childhood holidays and on a subliminal level it haunted his memory.

This year Smithson chose to fly with Andrea, Veronica and Knayler to his place on Bighorn Lake near the Montana border in Wyoming and he was glad that he had. He loved this ranch. It was one of his first. He had come in search of a place in this part of the country years before because of his admiration of Crazy Horse. On June 25, 1876, just over fifty miles northeast of the ranch, the great Lakota warrior and his allies had wiped out the megalomaniacal General George Armstrong Custer and his men.

Though it had snowed during the previous night, this morning was sunny and rather warm for late December. When Smithson led his wife, daughter and Knayler out to the barn and showed them the four palominos he had bought for them all, he could not have been happier at the delight that they displayed at the sight of the beautiful tan and white horses. It was decided that they would go riding as soon as appropriate attire could be changed into and Smithson asked a ranch hand, a man named Larry Skylar, who he was paying triple time to be there for the morning, to saddle the animals and prepare to lead them on their ride.

"This is the best Christmas *ever!*" exclaimed Veronica, as they walked back to the house. She was literally jumping for joy.

"It really is, Phil," agreed Andrea, tugging on his right arm and giving him a loud, wet kiss on the cheek.

"I've never had a horse before," said Knayler, who shook his head and looked as if he could barely believe that he now did have one. "Thanks, Sport."

"Neither have I, Bird. And you're more than welcome," said Smithson. "I'm glad everyone is happy. This *is* the best Christmas ever."

100.

Sins Of The Father

"There have been very few people who have fully understood who Bryant Smithson really was, Paul." Randall Cook and Paul had retired to the confines of Jeff's studio after a perfect Christmas celebration. Paul had told Randall that he knew he was bound to not betray any confidences, but that he believed there were things in Phillip Smithson's past that were now effecting his judgment, things that Randall might know about and be willing to share with Paul, so that he could better assess a situation that he believed might be developing. Paul discreetly avoided saying that he believed that Randall had been an intelligence agent, knowing that Randall would either be aware of something relevant and be willing to share it or not. In turn, Randall did not ask what business a retired FBI agent would have with "a situation" involving Phillip Smithson. Paul had stated that he believed Smithson had served in the special forces in Vietnam, maybe the Phoenix Program, but that he suspected there was something else of importance in his history, something he might resent. Randall hadn't confirmed Paul's belief about Smithson's Vietnam service, but he hadn't denied it either. "But he was the chairman of the Senate Armed Services Committee between 1958 and 1963, so it was necessary for certain elements of the government to know everything possible about him."

"I understand," said Paul.

"Most everything there is to know about the liberal Senator

from Massachusetts is a matter of public record. It's no secret that he came from a family of East Boston merchants. They were better off than most people, but by no means wealthy. He had higher ambitions. He studied hard, got a scholarship to Harvard, where he majored in business and made a lot of important connections. He worked nights, weekends and summers in various family businesses. Now when I say that he made important connections at Harvard, don't get the idea that he made a lot of friends. Bryant Smithson never really had many of what you and I would call 'friends'. He was someone who apparently looked at everybody as someone who either was or was not useful to his ambitions. He was a born deal maker, Paul, and if he believed there might be something to gain from a relationship, then he would make the effort to form a relationship. If not, well…"

"I know the type," said Paul.

"Of course. Not at all uncommon. On the surface he was extremely personable, built a reputation as a do-gooder, volunteering to work for charities, and, once he'd made a little money as a real estate developer, he was sure to make it known that he donated rather generously to them, as well.

"Eventually he met Rosemary Carton, daughter of the former governor, Nathaniel Carton, and if his ambitions had not been political all along, it became obvious after their marriage, that with the connections he now had through his father-in-law, they were now *entirely* political. Now, there are those who have speculated that a handsome young fellow like Bryant Smithson, well on his way to financial affluence, who could have had his pick of lovely young ladies… he'd had relationships with several who were more beautiful and from wealthier families… chose to wed Rosemary, who was rather plain and, though not crippled by it, had a bit of a hunched back, due to scoliosis… that he chose to wed Rosemary only because she was Nathaniel Carton's daughter."

"Yes," Paul said. "I've heard this said about him before, but…"

Randall held up his hand, silencing Paul. "But what is a well hidden secret may well be the answer to what you're looking for. Bryant and Rosemary made several attempts to have children before Phillip was born, all resulting in miscarriages. Phillip was born in Paris in October of 1948. Did you know that?"

"Yes, I'm aware of that," answered Paul.

"Ah. But what you are not aware of is that by this time it had been determined that Rosemary would most likely never be able to bring a pregnancy to term."

"So…"

"So Phillip is Bryant's son, but he is not Rosemary's."

101.

Life Support

When Paul opened his laptop the following morning, the first thing to catch his eye on the CBS homepage came as a shock. There in a window in the top left hand corner of the screen was Veronica Smithson's high school yearbook picture with a headline beneath it reading: Smithson Daughter on Life Support. He clicked on the headline and read the story.

It said that Veronica had been thrown from a horse that had been spooked by a rabbit, while riding with her parents on Christmas morning at their ranch on Bighorn Lake, west of Lovell, Wyoming. She had landed on her head, knocking her unconscious and breaking her neck. It appeared that she was now completely paralyzed and was breathing with the assistance of a respirator at West Park Hospital in Cody, Wyoming. She had not regained consciousness and her prognosis was far from positive. Her mother and father were at her side and had given no statement to the press, but had apparently asked a family friend, one Gary Knayler, who had been with them at the time of the accident, to say that they knew Veronica was in everyone's hearts and prayers.

Paul knew that the nature of horses' eyes causes them to exaggerate the size of things, but he found himself wondering about the idea of a little rabbit frightening such a large animal and it just seemed incredible to him. Then he thought of Jeff lying in his hospital bed years before and how he and Joan had feared for his recovery. He could not help but feel profound sympathy for

Phillip and Andrea Smithson. He said a silent prayer for them and their daughter, sighed and stared at the girl's picture. She was so young and innocent looking, with a radiant smile that seemed to broadcast nothing so much as it did youthful optimism and Paul felt guilty that he was now taking it for granted that she would not survive.

102.

Phoenix

In Vietnam, Phillip Smithson had served as Tom McAdams's lieutenant in the Phoenix Program, the CIA's secret assassinations program. On their last mission, both had nearly been killed and McAdams had been captured. McAdams had spent the rest of the war in the notorious Vietnamese prison, the Hanoi Hilton, and Smithson had been hospitalized for months, first in Saigon and later in the V.A. hospital in West Los Angeles, California.

Smithson had killed dozens of people in Vietnam and had murdered six serial killers in the United States since McAdams's death without ever feeling a shred of guilt about his actions. He was not a man without a conscience. He had simply rationalized everything he had done as having been justifiably necessary, but as he sat watching his daughter lying in a hospital bed, breathing only because a machine was making it possible, he remembered the only woman he had ever killed, a beautiful Vietnamese villager, who had hid caches of weapons, ammunition and other supplies for the Viet Cong and who had been functioning as a spy for them, reporting everything she could learn about the activities of U.S. and South Vietnamese forces in the area around her village. She had been no older than his daughter now was when Smithson had garroted her.

In classical mythology, the phoenix was a great bird that lived for five or six centuries in the Arabian desert, after which it burned itself on a funeral pyre, then rose from the ashes with renewed youth to live through another cycle. It made no logical sense, but as

Smithson sat looking at the girl he loved more than anyone else in the world, he wished he could give back the Vietnamese woman's life as payment for Veronica's recovery, for he felt certain, just as he knew the woman's resurrection was impossible, that nothing short of a miracle would allow his daughter's life to not slip away and, for the first time since he had taken a human life, he felt guilty, guilty of killing a beautiful young Vietnamese woman on a moonless, winter night in 1972. In his mind's eye he saw himself lowering the woman's lifeless body onto the mat on which she had been sleeping and he was thankful that his wife had left the room minutes earlier, for he began to weep.

103.

Gary Knayler

Investigating Gary Knayler's history, Paul learned that he had been born Gary MacPherson Knayler in Oden, Arkansas on April 22, 1945, the fourth of Henry and Hilda Knayler's seven children, and raised there on the bank of the Ouachita River in the heart of the Ouachita National Forest. His father was a game warden, but he'd also owned a gas station and garage and Gary, who had shown an aptitude for mechanics early on, had worked there from the age of eleven, tirelessly repairing cars and commuting twenty miles during the school year to Mt. Ida, where he'd attended Mt. Ida High School. Immediately upon graduation from high school, he'd packed up the 1940 Ford Opera Coupe he had restored from the ground up and driven to Wichita, Kansas, where he'd enrolled in airplane mechanic school. Before long he was taking flying lessons and flying soon became his passion. In late August of 1965, he'd joined the army with the promise that he'd be trained to fly helicopters and the following spring found him doing just that in the skies over South Vietnam.

Paul found that Knayler's service record wasn't classified. He'd served eight years in the army, mostly in Vietnam, and had survived being shot down twice and one crash due to apparent mechanical failure. He'd been discharged as a captain in 1973 with a long list of decorations and soon after his return to The States he'd become an instructor at The Bluebird School of Aviation, a small flight school in St. Petersburg, Florida. In June of 1974 he'd become the private pilot for Lancaster DeVille, the Tampa based real estate tycoon, but when DeVille was indicted for fraud in December of that same year, Knayler had found himself out of a job. A month later he'd been arrested at the airport in New Orleans on suspicion of smuggling marijuana, but the charges were later dropped for lack of evidence. Spring of 1975 found him back in St. Petersburg teaching flying at Bluebird.

In September of 1975 he'd met Mary Anne Greenwich, when she'd begun taken flying lessons from him, and in March of the following year they were married. His boss decided to retire later that year and he'd been sufficiently enamored with Gary to co-sign a loan so that Knayler could buy his business. Gary and Mary Anne had run the flight school successfully until they sold it in 1989 and moved to Nevada where Knayler had then begun working as Phillip Smithson's private pilot.

What Paul couldn't know from his investigation of Knayler was that he was a person who related to the world in an almost entirely physical way. Under other circumstances, he might have been a champion athlete. He could juggle like a circus performer. He could mentally picture the most intricate machinery functioning in three dimensions from an early age and, had he chosen to, could have flourished as a mechanical engineer. He was an expert hunter and he could have, while blindfolded, disassembled and reassembled any weapon with which he was familiar.

When he and Mary Anne were courting, she'd found him to be a natural on the dance floor, never needing a second instruction, no matter how detailed or difficult the routine. Knayler would tell her that flying a helicopter was like dancing. It required the co-ordinated use of both hands and both feet and a pilot had to become one with the machine to really master it. Perhaps only Mary Anne ever fully appreciated just how much Gary needed to be interacting with something or someone at all times in order to feel complete and how he cherished his relationships with all things and persons with which he could successfully mesh. She judged there to be no more loyal man on Earth and observed how he could fall asleep anywhere in a few moments simply by disengaging himself from all interaction.

There was no record of Knayer and Smithson's first meeting, precisely because it occurred when Smithson was returning from a secret mission that officially never happened. The second time Knayler was shot down he'd been flying alone back to his base when Viet Cong AK-47 fire disabled his Huey, but he'd managed to autorotate and come down softly in a clearing in the jungle canopy. The Huey that had extracted Smithson and Tom McAdams from a landing zone several klicks from their covert action just happened to be in the immediate vicinity when Knayler sent a mayday message saying that he was going down. It was followed by a second transmission in which he said he was down safely but drawing fire. Smithson and McAdams exchanged knowing looks, then insisted their pilot head for where Knayler had crashed. When they arrived they also began to draw heavy fire, too heavy to consider landing or even remaining close, so they flew two hundred yards away before Smithson and McAdams descended droplines to the jungle floor and made their way back through the jungle towards Knayler, where, in the course of the next hour, they killed seven Viet Cong before pulling the by then wounded pilot to the roof of his Huey, from which they where all extracted.

104.

New Year's Eve

Efraim Gutierrez made his living as the lead guitarist in a Latin rock band, that was based in Baton Rougue, Louisiana, called Los Extranjeros. His hero was Carlos Santana and his greatest thrill was having jammed with the great man at a party, where Los Extranjeros were providing the music, in the summer of 2003 in New Orleans, when Carlos consented to join them on stage for their rendition of *Oye Como Va*. Efraim was engaged at the time to his lovely high school sweetheart, Doreen Boisseau, and they were intending to get married in September. They were deeply in love and Doreen could not have been prouder of Efraim for pursuing and succeeding at his dream of being a professional musician.

Though Efraim thought she looked just fine, Doreen wanted to lose fifteen pounds before the wedding and she started taking diet pills. They seemed to help some, but she found she still had an appetite for all of the excellent cuisine where she was working as a waitress, especially the rich and fattening desserts, and when a friend suggested trying a hit of crystal meth one afternoon, she gave it a try. Soon she was hooked on the drug and Efraim found that nothing he could do, no amount of love, begging or threats, could tear her away from it and get her clean. Before long the relationship was over and Doreen lost her place to live. Then she lost her job. Eventually she turned to prostitution.

On New Year's Eve, Efraim found himself awaiting trial on attempted murder charges, after a rowdy, drunken Louisiana State

University sophomore kicked in Los Extranjeros' drummer's bass drumhead at a frat party where they'd been playing and the whole band had wound up brawling with most of the frat boys. By the time the police arrived, Efraim had stabbed the young man who had kicked the drumhead in and he was taken away in handcuffs and booked for attempted murder.

Weeks went by as he remained in custody and now, as 2009 approached, he thought he saw his opportunity as Micky Landis, in shackles and chains, was being escorted by a guard back to his cell toward him, while Efraim was being led to the telephone room, and, quick as lightning, he double-stepped, extended his lower right leg behind Micky's right calf, while throwing his right palm under Micky's chin, he tore him from his escort and smashed his skull on the concrete floor, before either his or Micky's guard could react. When they did react he went limp, offering no resistance whatsoever, for he was satisfied that he had done what he had plotted all along to do. He had finally caught up with and killed the man who had murdered his dear Doreen.

Several hours later, at one minute after midnight in Cody, Wyoming, Veronica Smithson's heart stopped beating.

105.

Condolences

Paul briefly considered attending Veronica's funeral service, just as he had thought about confronting Smithson at times during the previous week. He knew the man would be at his most vulnerable, but he could not bring himself to that level of brutality. So he simply sent flowers and a note that read: My wife and I wish to express our sincere condolences. What I know you have been through I would not wish on anyone. He addressed it only to Phillip Smithson and signed it with his name alone.

Paul knew that Smithson would wonder why the note had not been addressed to both himself and his wife and why it had not been signed with both Paul's and his wife's names. He looked forward to a response.

106.

Funeral In The Desert

People have a wide variety of ideas about the meaning of life and the finality of death and perhaps a majority of people are of the opinion that death is not actually the end of life at all, but simply a new beginning. Some believe in an afterlife, an eternal spiritual life in heaven or hell. Others believe in reincarnation, returning in a new form to live again on Earth as a different person or animal.

Phillip Smithson believed death was like crossing the edge of the universe into an eternal void, that there was nothing at all after one's life ended, no joy or suffering, no awareness, no rebirth and certainly no God. Andrea, however, had held onto what her father had told her as a child, that her mother was now with The Great Spirit, the giver of life, and her ancestors, forever watching over her from heaven. She was aware that she believed this because she wanted to believe it and that it may be a naïve sentiment, but she also believed that it was preferable to the hopelessness that she thought was inherent in the belief that death was the absolute end. While raising Veronica, she had told the child of her beliefs and the girl had adopted them as her own before finding, while in high school, that she preferred the idea of reincarnation.

Andrea remembered that, during one of their last conversations on the subject, Veronica had told her that her belief in reincarnation had made her unafraid of dying and that, when her time came, she would want to be cremated, to have her ashes scattered from a plane over the desert and for her funeral to be a celebration of her life. So, although Veronica's premature death had shattered both of her parents, Andrea told her husband that they should do their best to fulfill their daughter's wishes. She said it would be the best thing for Veronica's friends, as well, and probably the best thing they could do for themselves too, in an effort to find acceptance in the face of this overpowering loss. Phillip listened and acquiesced. He believed in his wife's good judgment, knew that Veronica's friends would probably benefit from this approach and, though personally he was so devastated that he thought he'd never recover at all and would rather be dead himself than to have his daughter gone, he was in too weakened a state to even think of any reason to disagree.

The service took place at ten o'clock on the morning of January fourth. As popular as Veronica and her parents were, both Phillip and Andrea were still astonished at the hundreds of people who converged on the location in the desert they had chosen for the ceremony. Andrea's cousin, Wolf's Ear, an Apache medicine man and Veronica's favorite relative, presided. He spoke about Veronica's desire that her life be celebrated at this time, how she had been so talented and bright, how she had been so well loved by everyone who knew her. He said that she believed she would return to live in a new body again and again and that, therefore, her life would go on and on. He said that they should all respect her beliefs and that she was wise beyond her years. Then, as one of her favorite songs, R. Kelly's *I Believe I Can Fly*, was played over a set of huge stereo speakers, sitting at either end of the dais, a vintage, red, Stearman biplane flew over the crowd, banked to the east and Gary Knayler, sitting in its rear seat, scattered Veronica's ashes from the starboard side of the open cockpit and, as they dispersed, directly behind them a bolt of lightning flashed to the ground from the storm clouds that were gathering over the hills to the north.

Both Phillip and Andrea were taken aback by the spontaneous cheering that erupted from Veronica's mourners at the sight of this, then Andrea began to weep. Phillip let go of her hand, put his arm around her, squeezed her shoulder and said, "It's alright, baby. It's alright."

"Oh Phil," she responded, smiling serenely through her tears, "this is so right. I'm so glad we did this. This is what she wanted."

"Yes, it is. Thank-you for making me understand that."

107.

Darwin

Hans Newfield liked to tell the girls he'd take on outings to Kakadu National Park the story of how his family had come to live in Australia in 1955. He didn't know every detail, but it mattered little. He was a skilled liar and knew how to make it sound entertaining.

His grandfather, Fritz Neumeier, was a talented twenty-four-year-old dental student when the Nazis invaded Poland, so he was happy to learn that The Fatherland valued his skills enough that he would not be required to serve with a combat unit when he was conscripted into the German army in 1939. He spent most of the war in the concentration camp at Buchenwald, removing gold fillings from the teeth of inmates before they were sent to the gas chamber and he discovered that, once in a while, he was able to pocket one or two. He squirreled them away in a bottle of molasses that he kept locked in his footlocker. On the rare occasions when he was given a leave of absence, he would take the bottle and send it to his wife, Gertraude, in Hannover, with strict instructions to hide it on the back of the top shelf of a kitchen cabinet and to tell no one about it, not even their little son, Rudi.

It was the morning of December 10, 1942, when a Colonel, who was suffering from a severe toothache, took offense at what he perceived to be a less than formal salute from Neumeier upon the senior officer's arrival. When Neumeier apologized, the Colonel was unconvinced of his sincerity. Things went from bad to worse. Neumeier carefully probed the Colonel's tooth while the man winced. Neumeier was growing nervous. His probe found a nerve and the officer howled and thrust the dentist's arm away. A tear rolled down the Colonel's cheek and he wiped it away. Neumeier apologized again and explained that the tooth was hopeless and would have to come out. The Colonel was red-faced behind the hand that he held to his jaw.

"Gibt es kein anderer Zahnarzt in diesem verdammten Lager?!" he demanded. *Is there no other dentist in this damned camp?!*

"Ja, selbstverstandlich, Herr Oberst," answered Neumeier. *Yes, of course, Herr Colonel.*

"Erhalten Sie ihn!" ordered the Colonel. *Get him!*

Neumeier excused himself and went in search of his immediate superior, Dr. Schrenk. The Colonel would be Neumeier's last patient at Buchenwald. The next morning he found that he had been reassigned. Orders had been issued that he was to be sent to serve with a unit outside of Stalingrad, where the Germans had been struggling since July to take the city from the Russians. While en route, he managed to send the final bottle of molasses to his wife, with word that, should she hear he had been killed or captured, she should take little Rudi and the gold and try to get to his cousin Elsie's place in Flensburg and from there to do whatever she could to get across the border to Denmark to await the end of the war.

Rudi Neumeier was seventeen years old when he next saw his father, upon his release from the U.S.S.R. in 1955. Though Fritz was only thirty-nine, he looked to be at least fifty-five. His hair was white as snow and he walked with the aid of a cane. Gertraude would perhaps not have recognized him when he stepped from his train in Hamburg, had he not had the foresight to send her a photograph the previous week. But it was a miracle that he had survived at all. The great majority of the German prisoners taken by the Russians had not and had Fritz Neumeier not possessed the useful skills of a dentist, he knew he would not have lived to see Germany again either.

Gertraude had always had faith that her husband would return, though, even through all of the years when there had been no word that he was even alive. She had managed to flee with Rudi to Denmark after hearing that Fritz had been taken prisoner not long after the Germans began their retreat from Stalingrad and she had done so without needing to part with any of the gold. Life was very hard in Germany after the war, but they had remained in Denmark, where she had found work as a dental assistant. They had been just fine.

Fritz was very glad to hear all of this and amazed to hear that the gold still sat in the molasses bottles, on a top shelf of her kitchen cabinets in Copenhagen. Soon after the family's arrival in Copenhagen, however, Fritz began to show signs of paranoia. Once he'd learned of the fate of the Nazis who had been tried at Nuremberg, he began to fear that his role at Buchenwald would be found out and he began to have nightmares about Jews who had survived the war coming in search of the gold fillings in the dead of night. He soon found he could no longer face going out in the street. He was convinced that sooner or later someone was bound to recognize him and he'd be made to face the consequences. He told his wife there was only one thing to do and that they would have to do it: they would use the gold to finance a move to Australia. Rudi was reluctant; it would mean leaving behind everything he knew, including his girlfriend. However, Gertraude loved his father; when she looked in his eyes, she saw the same man she had known and adored before the war. Rudi loved his mother. He agreed to go. Gertraude and Rudi spoke English fluently and had once even vacationed in London. Fritz would learn. He'd picked up the difficult Russian language easily, after all.

Within weeks they arrived in Darwin, on the north coast of Australia. They were now Doctor and Mrs. Emil Neufeld and son, Rudolf, better known as Rudi. Using the credentials of Gertraude's employer as a guide and with the help of a friend of Gertraude's, who was a printer, it had not been difficult to obtain forged documents for Dr. Emil Neufeld. Before very long he had a growing dental practice in Darwin.

Usually near this point in his narrative, Hans would be asked how his name came to be Newfield and he would explain that his father, Rudi, had anglicized his name in 1964, when he formed his band, Rudy Newfield and The Newsmen, after The Beatles caused a worldwide sensation and every boy and young man on Earth who could sing, or play a guitar, keyboards or the drums, tried his hand at joining or creating a band. Rudy played a Hammond B3 organ and was the lead vocalist in his.

"The band that did *Kangaroo Courtship*?!" his companions would sometimes ask.

Hans would roll his eyes and say, "Yes, and it reached number one on the Australian charts."

The girls who let it go at that were the lucky ones, but often instead, they'd get excited and say things like, "Wow! Rudy Newfield was a big star! They still play his stuff on the radio! My mom had all of his records! I can't believe he was your father!" etc., and this would be the beginning of the end for them, for the more they raved, the more his blood pressure would rise.

Rudy Newfield *was* a big star, one of the biggest to come out of Australia in the 1960s at least, for not only did his biggest hit, *Kangaroo Courtship*, reach number one in Australia in 1965, the album it was on did too and they both did very well in America

and The U.K. Plus, though he'd never attain quite such great success again, the band recorded seven more albums that sold reasonably well over the following four years and they toured the world
twice. Then Rudy formed his next venture, The New, with whom
he recorded ten albums in six years, had a hit with an instrumental
version of the Jimi Hendrix song, *Can You See Me?*, which made
the top ten in the U.S., Canada, The U.K., Germany, Australia
and Japan in 1971, and did three world tours. In 1976 came The
New Newsmen, whose three albums sold relatively poorly, though
the title tune to their first one, *Jamaica Mistake?*, climbed as high
as number fifteen on the Australian charts and they packed in the
crowds in concert, where they covered the more popular tunes
of the first two bands, before they disbanded in March of 1979.
Rudy took a long break and began spending his time at home in
Darwin with his wife, Rebecca, and his two-year-old son, Hans,
who he eventually took to severely beating when the boy would
not stop wetting his bed, while Hans would hope against hope
that his mother would intervene, but she never did. Finally, in late
1982, Rudy recorded a solo album, *Unified Newfield Theory*, which
enjoyed critical acclaim. The track *Rudy Awakening* did well enough
in the charts worldwide that a world tour was launched and on the
snowy night of October 18, 1983, in Alberta, Canada, came the
plane crash that elevated Rudy to the status of a dead rock god.
Two albums were released posthumously. Over the years *The Best
Of Rudy Newfield* sold better than any of his other albums, because
it sells fairly well to this day. A Christmas album, *Hams and Yams*,
released for Christmas of 1983, is widely accepted as having been
recorded just for family and friends, with Rudy soloing on piano
and vocals, during a Christmas party at his home in 1982. The
hilarious *Drunk Russian Woman*, from that album, did very well
worldwide and reached number five in Australia.

By the time of Rudy's death, Hans had found he'd acquired a taste for lighting fires, throwing rocks through windows, torturing every little animal he could get his hands on and bullying other children. Eventually he stopped the rock throwing.

Between October of 2003 and January of 2009, seventeen women between the ages of eighteen and twenty-six, who had briefly known Hans Newfield, had vanished from an area within a hundred kilometers of Darwin. It made the news nationwide and then worldwide, but the authorities were stumped. They would remain so, because Hans wasn't going to enlighten them and neither were the crocodiles to which he'd fed his victims.

108.

Smithson's Reply

When the Smithsons' reply came, a week after Veronica's service, it was addressed to Mr. and Mrs. Paul Warren. In distinctly feminine handwriting it read: Our daughter's spiritual belief was that all life is eternal. We know that she will live on in the hearts and minds of all who knew and loved her. Thank-you for your kindness. Andrea Smithson had signed it: Phillip and Andrea Smithson.

After reading it, Paul called Backdoor Bobby to get the latest results of Bobby's ongoing monitoring of Phillip Smithson's online activity.

109.

Bailey

Phillip Smithson sat at the desk in the knotty pine walled study of his house at Bighorn Lake, opened a box of .45 caliber cartridges and extracted one. He closed the box and set it on the blotter before him. Then he picked up an antique, nickel plated, Colt single action army revolver from the blotter, opened its cylinder, loaded the single round into a chamber and snapped the cylinder closed. He looked at the gun in his hand. Veronica had given it to him as a Christmas gift only two weeks earlier. He looked to the window and saw the sunshine sparkling on the enormous icicles that were hanging from the eves outside.

When he stood up he saw that he had tracked snow across the study's carpet and it was now melting. He looked down at his boots. No matter, he thought; it's only water. He proceeded to the door of the study and crossed the large living room, past its big stone fireplace and pushed open the swinging door to the kitchen. He walked across the kitchen, opened the door to the back porch, stepped out, closed the door and stood looking at the barn through his breath as it froze in the air of the cold Wyoming morning. He was just stepping down the stairs when he heard an engine roaring in the distance to his right and he looked to see a pickup truck coming down the snow covered road that led to the house and barn from his north gate. He knew right away that it would be Larry Skylar. He put the gun in the pocket of his sheepskin coat and continued on toward the barn. He waited by the barn door for Skylar to pull up and get out of his truck.

"Everything alright, boss? Wasn't expecting you to be here." The way Skylar said it, the second line sounded as much like a question as the first. He'd flown to Las Vegas for Veronica's service and Smithson had said nothing to him about coming to Wyoming any time soon.

"Yeah, Larry. It was a spur of the moment decision to fly up. I wasn't exactly expecting you either."

Skylar's first reaction was to say: you city folks. He caught himself, however, and simply said, "Them horses need lookin' after. Gotta be fed. Stalls need muckin' out."

"Oh, of course," said Smithson. "Say, Larry. Would you mind doing me a favor first though?"

"I work for you, Mr. Smithson. Whatever it is, you just name it."

"Would you get a fire going in the living room for me?"

"Sure, boss. Nothin' to it." Skylar started off toward the back porch and Smithson took hold of the knob to the barn's pedestrian door. Skylar stopped and turned around.

"Boss?"

Smithson turned to face him. "Yes?"

"I know I told you before, Mr. Smithson, but I sure am sorry."

"I know, Larry," said Smithson nodding. "I know you are."

Smithson then opened the barn door, went inside and closed the door behind himself. Skylar watched him go, then turned to go and build a fire in the living room.

Smithson went to the stall of the horse that had thrown his daughter, finding a coiled rope hanging on a peg nearby, in which he fashioned a slip knot. He was surprised to find that Skylar had screwed a brass plate to the stall's gate with the name Veronica had decided to give her horse: Bailey. He took an apple from the left hand pocket of his coat and held it up before the gate. All four horses had shown an immediate interest in his approach, but now this one eagerly stuck its head beyond the gate, as Smithson made it pursue the apple. He easily passed the loop in the rope over the horse's head and secured it around its neck. Then he unlatched the gate, swung it open and led the horse from its stall to the back door of the barn. He unlatched the big door and rolled it open, then led the horse through it and over to a corral fence, to which he tied the loose end of the rope.

As he took the Colt from his pocket, he noticed that the only sound he could hear was the horse's breathing. Then there was the crunch of his boots in the snow, as he approached the horse. He raised the gun and aimed it at the center of its forehead. The palomino looked at him, but didn't stir.

He was just about to squeeze the trigger when he had the distinct feeling that he was being watched by someone other than the horse. He lowered the gun and turned to look at the barn. No one. He slowly turned a full 360 degrees, carefully scanning in every direction with the skill of a practiced hunter, but he didn't see another living thing. Again he raised the revolver and aimed it at the horse's forehead. He thought of Veronica climbing onto the animal's back and how delighted she had been that morning.

Once again he had the feeling he was being watched, this time even stronger than before. He lowered the gun and again began to look around. To the north he saw a lone bird take to the sky from a treetop and begin flying in his direction. He watched it until it circled over head, then flew down to the corral and lighted on the fence only ten feet from where he had tied the rope, where it sat and looked at him, then at the horse, then back at him. It was shiny black. He thought it was a raven. It didn't make a sound, but just stared at him and, as he imagined it were asking him just what in the world he thought he was doing, he realized he was hiding the gun from it behind his right hip. He put the Colt back in his pocket and the bird began to flap its wings and right away flew directly back in the direction from which it had come. As he watched it go, Smithson remembered the song that had been played as his daughter's ashes had fallen and drifted in the sky above the desert, with its lyrics:

I believe I can fly
I believe I can touch the sky
I think about it every night and day
Spread my wings and fly away

"Boss?" he heard Skylar say behind him and turned to see the man in the door of the barn. "Is everything alright?"

Smithson turned away from him and looked at the horse. "Yes, Larry. Everything is fine," he answered, as he felt the Colt in his pocket.

"I got that fire going. Anything else you want me to do before I tend to these animals?" asked Skylar.

"No, Larry, you do what you need to do," answered Smithson, then he turned and started towards the barn. "When you're finished though, there is something you could do for me. I want you to get rid of this horse."

"Get rid of it, sir?"

"Yes. Get rid of it. I don't care what you do with it. You can give it away or sell it to a dog food company. You can keep it yourself, but I never want to see it again." Smithson stopped as he got close to Skylar and looked him in the eye. "I want it off this property this morning, understand?"

"Sure thing, boss. Consider it done."

"Alright then," said Smithson, as he walked away through the barn. "Thank-you."

He exited through the pedestrian door, went to the house and unloaded the Colt, locked it in his desk, then immediately departed for the airport.

110.

V.I.P. Treatment

Late in the morning, a day after Phillip Smithson returned to Las Vegas, Paul arrived at the GBC Building and was somewhat surprised to find that he was treated like royalty.

Not only was everyone familiar with exactly who he was from his work on the Andrew Travis Johansen case, which he realized was only normal, but, from the moment he stepped up to the reception desk in the second floor lobby, he found they couldn't seem to do enough to accommodate him.

He told a pretty, red haired woman behind the reception desk that he had come to study their serial killer database.

"Certainly, Agent Warren," she replied. He didn't bother to tell her he was no longer with the FBI. "Those files are open to the public, though I expect of course that they'd be made available to you even if they were not." She pushed a button on a telephone console as she was saying this. "If you'd like to have a seat, I'll have someone with you in just a moment to escort you to our library."

He thanked her, carried his attaché case to an assemblage of black leather couches and chairs surrounding a glass and stainless steel coffee table and sat on the couch that faced the reception desk. He reached for a magazine on the table with Andrea Smithson's picture on its cover, but before he could touch it he heard his name being called and looked up to see a lanky, blonde man in his late twenties, wearing a light blue western style suit, a leather string bolo tie with a sterling silver Zuni dancer inlaid with turquoise, black and white onyx and red oyster shell and tan cowboy boots, striding across the lobby toward him. The man had the toothiest smile Paul thought he'd ever seen. Paul stood to meet his outstretched hand as the man exclaimed, with an accent that Paul judged to be West Texan, "Welcome to GBC, Agent Warren! I'm Burton Perry. Very pleased to meet you, sir!" He pumped Paul's arm firmly.

"My pleasure."

"Kathy tells me you've come to see our serial murderer files." Perry's smile was dazzling and appeared to be sincere. Paul couldn't help but picture him on a horse and wearing a white ten-gallon hat.

"Yes. That's right."

"I hope you haven't come all the way from Virginia just to examine them; the entire database is accessible online at our website, as is everything we've ever broadcast, including every special segment on serial killers from *What's Wrong With This Picture?*" His concern seemed to be genuine.

"I had other business to attend to in the area, so I thought I'd come right to the source."

"Good decision! If you'll come with me, we'll make you feel right at home."

Perry led Paul to a bank of elevators, one of which they took to the fourth floor, then down a short hallway to an oaken office door, making small talk all the while about Paul's trip, his hotel accommodations and the magnificent Vegas weather.

"We normally make our computer library available to visitors, but I think you'd be more comfortable with a private office," Perry explained as he led Paul inside and with a sweep of his arm presented to him the desk, with a computer and telephone, a counter along one wall, with a coffee maker on top, a refrigerator below and cabinets on the wall above, a tan leather couch, and the view through the large, tinted window.

"Oh, I don't want to be any trouble..."

"No trouble at all, sir! It's the least we can offer a V.I.P. and I'm sure you wouldn't want to be disturbed with the distractions of the library," Perry said, dismissing the idea of trouble with a wave of his left hand, as he brought the computer to life and accessed GBC's website with his right.

"Well then..."

"Just make yourself comfortable. Is a PC okay? I can give you an office with an Apple if you'd prefer."

"PC is just fine."

"Terrific. Now, what would you like for refreshment? There's bottled water and coffee making supplies here at all times, of course, but we'd like you to take full advantage of our kitchen. And before you object, it's no trouble at all."

"Well, since you insist, a coke with no ice would be nice."

"Coke with no ice. I'll have one sent up right away and I'll leave you to your work, but first, while I'm insisting I'd like to insist that you order some lunch when your coke arrives. We've got everything and it's all excellent, so please don't hesitate."

"Well, alright. Thank-you, Mr. Perry."

"Please; it's nothing. And please call me Burton."

"Thank-you, Burton."

"You're more than welcome, sir. Have a productive afternoon," Perry wished him as he was closing the office door.

"Oh, Burton," Paul stopped him.

"Yes, sir?" Perry peeked back in.

"How late are you open?"

"The majority of the personnel leave at five, but we're a twenty-four hour operation three hundred and sixty-five days a year. You, sir, are welcome to stay around the clock, if you wish."

"Thank-you, Burton."

Perry gave him the okay sign and closed the door.

When he'd gone, Paul looked out the window at the Luxor pyramid in the distance, then he placed his attaché case on the desk, opened it and extracted a pen and a yellow legal pad from beneath a smaller case, which held his Les Baer 1911 automatic, sat down at the desk and began his examination of GBC's serial killer files.

111.

Salty

Gregor MacKushgy was the chief of security for GBC. Everyone called him Salty, going back to his days as a merchant seaman. At sixteen he'd left an abusive home in Edinburg, Scotland and got a job on a freighter, after convincing a skeptical freight crew chief that he could easily lift over his head more than his weight in a crate or burlap sack of goods and hold it there as long as he pleased. He was rather short, but strong as a bull and nearly as tough as one. Eight months later, when his ship went down in a hurricane off the coast of South Carolina, MacKushgy managed to don a survival suit and, as he was tossed on the sea beneath the thunder and lightning, he promised the Lord above he'd never set foot on another boat, if he was allowed to live, but dedicate himself to a new land-based career where he could use his brains as well as his brawn. He had always been both clever and suspicious, so, after he was rescued, when he saw an ad in a newspaper for a private detective agency seeking trainees, he made an appointment and went and applied for the job. At first they were reluctant to consider hiring one so young, but he did look older than his seventeen years, so after he'd scored highly on the aptitude tests he was given, the agency had decided to give him a chance. Twenty years later, when Phillip Smithson was looking for a security chief, he'd been his company's top field agent for many years, but he'd grown bored with what was mostly surveillance work for insurance companies and spouses suspicious that their mates were cheating and Smithson was offering over twice what he was making with the agency, so when he was offered the job in Las Vegas, he'd accepted it and never regretted having done so. He loved his job and he prided himself on knowing every last little thing that happened at GBC.

Three and a half hours after Paul Warren had settled into an afternoon of studying GBC's serial killer database, MacKushgy took a break from the video surveillance screens in the GBC security office and picked up his phone to call Phillip Smithson.

"Mr. Smithson," he said, when Smithson answered, "it's Gregor MacKushgy."

"Salty. How are you? What's up?"

"I'm just fine, sir, but there's been an incident I thought you'd want to know about. Not a real big deal, but I know you always prefer to err on the side of caution, so I thought I should give you a ring and ask your advice."

"I have complete faith in you Salty. I'm sure you're doing the right thing. What's happened?"

"Well, a little over an hour ago, The Chest Of Gold downstairs threw a card player out of their place, who was winning at blackjack and they were convinced he was counting cards. He protested rather strongly when they asked him to leave and finally he took a swing at one of their boys when they insisted he go. The long and the short of it is that they tossed him in the alley and his face bounced off one of our Dumpsters and it knocked him out cold. I saw this all on a monitor and sent a couple of our guys down to check him out and when he came around and saw all the blood and realized his nose was broken, he told them to call an ambulance, which they did."

"Well, that's good."

"Yes, but when he'd been loaded aboard the ambulance and

they were about to close its doors, he shouted at one of our men, 'You'll be hearing from my lawyer!'"

"I'm glad you called me, Salty. I'll just give Keith Sawin in legal a call and I'm sure he'll know just what to do, if this guy wants to make trouble. Did you get his name?"

"Sorry to say I didn't, sir."

"That's alright. I'd guess there's only one card counter who's been pitched against one of our Dumpsters today."

"Thankfully, sir."

"Yes... well... Mr. Sawin will probably be calling you. You might want to be prepared to show him the video of the incident."

"Certainly, sir."

"Fine. So, how's every other little thing, Salty? No one's tried to take one of my computers home lately?" MacKushgy had caught a newly hired janitor trying to steal a computer during his first month at GBC.

"No sir," chuckled MacKushgy. "Not on my watch."

"I'm sure. Okay. Well, thanks again for the call, Salty. And you have a good day."

"Yes sir. Oh, sir, there is one more thing you may want to be aware of, as long as I've got you on the line. Mr. Warren, the former FBI man, came in shortly before noon to have a look at our serial killer files. Mr. Perry gave him an office on four."

Smithson didn't reply.

"Sir?" asked MacKushgy.

"Yes. Sorry, Salty. I was just switching ears. So... did he appear to be satisfied with what he saw?"

"Oh, he's still here, sir. Sorry I didn't make that clear."

"Still there after what, three and a half hours?" Smithson asked absently.

"Yes, sir. Bit more than that now."

"I wouldn't have thought we'd have that much information that he wasn't already familiar with," mused Smithson.

"Yes, well, perhaps the FBI hasn't given him open access to their stuff since he retired?"

"I s'pose," agreed Smithson. "Well, he's welcome to stay as long as he likes."

"I'm sure he's been told that, sir."

"Good. Great. Okay. Thanks, Salty. You be good now."

"Certainly, sir. Always. Take care, sir."

"Bye."

Both men hung up and MacKushgy left the security office to use the restroom, but Smithson didn't move from where he stood. He simply stared out the window of his kitchen and wondered what in the world Paul Warren didn't know that he could have already spent three and a half hours trying to find in GBC's files.

112.

The Steven Beck and
Jerome Anthony Anthony Files

Two things Paul was curious about were GBC's files on Steven Beck, who Paul was pretty certain was Smithson's first victim, and Jerome Anthony Anthony, the man from Santa Rosa, who Paul was sure Smithson had hunted down when no one else had even been aware that a serial killer had been active in the Santa Rosa area. He wanted to know when these files had originated and, more specifically, were there any indications that the files predated the men's deaths. As he'd expected, he found that there were no indications of that with either file.

The Anthony file appeared to have been compiled by GBC-News staff members as a history of the man and his victims, with the first entries having been made twelve days after his death. The only clues in the file that a serial murderer may have been operating in Santa Rosa prior to his death were copies of newspaper and internet stories about missing women, who subsequently turned out to be his victims, and missing persons reports on these same women, which had been filed with the police. Paul assumed that these missing persons reports had been provided by the people who had filed them with the police. He knew that the police department's own files were confidential. There were certainly no police files included in GBC's Anthony file concerning their investigations into the disappearances of missing women. The news stories, which had been published both before and after Anthony had been found, simply quoted police spokesmen saying that they were investigating or had investigated every lead, were seeking or had sought the public's help and were doing or had done everything they could. Paul knew, of course, that since no bodies had been discovered until after Anthony's body had been found, there had been no clear evidence that a serial killer was behind the disappearances, and since there had been nothing to indicate that the missing persons cases had involved the crossing of state lines and there was no actual evidence of kidnappings, the FBI had never been called in.

The Beck file appeared to have been compiled by GBCNews staffers, with the first entries having been made seven days after Captain Franklin Rhodes had closed the cases of Beck's victims and much of what Paul observed about the Anthony file could be said about the Beck file, as well. There were no police files included and it could be assumed that the missing persons reports were obtained from those who had filed them with the police. The police spokesman quoted in every news story, nearly all of which had been written by Edgar Biggleston, was Franklin Rhodes and before Steven Beck was found he'd said much the same as the Santa Rosa police had said about their missing women before their case was solved, that all leads were being investigated and that any help from the public would be appreciated. However, Paul was not surprised to find that the quotes from Rhodes after Beck and his victims were found seemed a bit more humanitarian than those of the Santa Rosa police spokesmen after Anthony and his victims were discovered. He showed sincere sympathy for the dead women and expressed great relief that the community's fears that a monster might be in their midst could finally be confirmed and allowed to dissipate. There were also news stories, again by Biggleston, about the two missing women who had, after all, not been killed by Beck, Amy Waterbury and Paulette Washburn. Paul was pleased to see that there was no mention of him anywhere in the Beck file. He had asked both Rhodes and Biggleston to keep his involvement confidential and they had respected his wishes.

All of GBC's serial killer files stated the cause of death of every victim and every murderer, if deceased. Paul was not surprised to see that Steven Beck's death was said to have been an accident and Jerome Anthony Anthony's a suicide, because he knew there were only two people who were aware they'd both actually been murdered and it was not, of course, in Phillip Smithson's best interest to correct these errors.

113.

The Arlen Wesley Henniford, Dennie Bordeaux, Kevin Pimental and Daniel David O'Reilly Files

Paul found that the Arlen Wesley Henniford and Dennie Bordeaux (now known as Dennis Frazier Bordeaux, since the media tended to refer to most people of great notoriety by their full names) files had begun as UNSUB files, consisting mostly of newspaper and internet stories about missing women and girls in New Jersey and Maine and speculation by law enforcement authorities that serial offenders were probably responsible for their disappearances. There were photographs of all of the victims and questions in large print asking HAVE YOU SEEN ANY OF THESE WOMEN? There were even maps showing the last known locations in which the women had been seen alive, just like the grids that Paul and his counterparts had routinely used to plot the comfort zones of abductors. Also there were 1-800 phone numbers and requests that readers call them should they believe they had any information that might be of assistance in finding the missing women.

In both cases, the killers' names and biographies were added to the files by GBCNews staffers within days after each of their deaths, once the authorities had made public clear evidence of their guilt.

The file that contained Kevin Pimental's name (he was generally referred to as "former attorney Kevin Pimental", though it was well known that his middle name was Charles) had also been originally assembled as an UNSUB file and it remained so. Pimental was said to be the prime suspect in the murders of the dead New Bedford area prostitutes, but no case had ever been proven. The authorities were in possession of nothing more linking him to the victims than they had been when they had dropped the case against him of Martine DeSimone's murder. Now that he was dead, they didn't hesitate to say that they believed he had been their killer, but they also made it clear that they may never be able to prove it.

Daniel David O'Reilly's file (he had always been known to the public at large as Daniel David O'Reilly) had first been assembled as an UNSUB file as well, but had been placed among the solved case files after Albany D.A. Santa Monica had made the announcement that O'Reilly had confessed to being "The Rte. 88 Ripper", a name that even the media, who had given it to him when he was still a mystery man, knew was a misnomer, as all of his victims had in fact been smothered and none had shown even the slightest sign of mutilation. O'Reilly's cause of death was reported as suicide by hanging, of course.

None of this came as a surprise to Paul. Before he'd left home he was long familiar with every scrap of information contained in the files except for who had assembled them for GBCNews and he hadn't expected to find any evidence that Smithson had had a hand in doing so. He had also assumed that he could have learned everything that he did learn from them on his home computer, but had chosen to do so at GBC specifically to let Smithson know he was doing it, hoping that the man might even monitor him, and moreover to be right there when Smithson chose to confront him.

114.

Curiosity

Late the following morning Smithson received a call from Keith Sawin, who assured him that they need not worry about the card counter. Sawin told him that the man's complaint, if there was to be one, was with The Chest Of Gold's security people and that if he contacted an attorney, any competent one would advise him of that fact. Smithson confirmed that Sawin had told Gregor MacKushgy this, then he thanked him and called MacKushgy.

"Salty, I just wanted to thank you again for staying on top of everything down there. It's a great comfort to know I can depend on your watchful eye."

"Just doing my job, sir."

"Well, it means a great deal to me."

"Don't give it a second thought, sir."

"Well, my point is that with you there I know I don't have to."

"Thank you, sir."

"By the way, what time did Mr. Warren finally leave last night?"

"I believe it was just after 9 PM, sir."

"Really, 9 PM? That's extraordinary! What in the world...?"

"And he was back at 8 this morning. He's here now, in fact."

"He is?"

"Indeed, sir. In the same office on the fourth floor. He just ordered a corned beef sandwich from the kitchen."

"I'll be damned," said Smithson. "I suppose the investigative staff should be flattered. Tell you what: if he's still around at 4 this afternoon, you let me know, okay? I'll have to ask him to have dinner with me and satisfy my curiosity."

"Certainly, sir."

"Okay, Salty. Thanks."

"My pleasure. Sir."

After he'd hung up with MacKushgy, Smithson called Burton Perry and asked what Paul Warren had specifically said he was interested in looking for. Perry told him that Warren had informed receptionist Kathy O'Hare that he had come to study their serial killer files and was no more specific with either her or himself. Perry also told Smithson that he'd informed Warren that the entire database and all of the *What's Wrong With This Picture?* telecasts were available online and that Warren's response was that he had other business to attend to locally and thought he'd therefore come right to the source. Smithson thanked Perry and hung up.

Smithson believed that Warren had to have known all along that he could have found everything online that he might find on a computer at GBC and that being in town on other business didn't change that fact. He thought about getting on his computer and monitoring what Warren was doing, then wondered if MacKushgy might have been doing that already. He wished that he had casually asked him to, but thought it might make him appear overanxious were he to ask him to do it now and the thought that MacKushgy might notice his own eavesdropping put him off the idea of doing it himself.

He began to wonder what Warren's other business might be and if it might be at GBC.

His mind was beginning to race. He checked his watch, then made himself a gin and tonic and told himself that there was really nothing to be concerned about, that Paul Warren was, after all, retired.

115.

Five After Four

By mid-afternoon on his first day at GBC, Paul had run out of things he felt he should check out in their files and since then he'd simply been watching serial killer segments from *What's Wrong With This Picture?*, while waiting for Phillip Smithson's curiosity to get the better of him. At five minutes after four o'clock in the afternoon of the second day, he was watching a scathing indictment of the St. Louis District Attorney's office and the deal that they'd allowed Andrew Michael Dunlop to make, which put him in a position to subsequently kill a deputy sheriff, when the phone on the desk rang. He paused the show and picked up the receiver on the third ring.

"Hello?"

"Agent Warren, this is Phil Smithson, how are you?"

"I'm just fine, Mr. Smithson. How are you?"

"Please call me Phil. We're not strangers."

"Okay, Phil," agreed Paul, knowing this was the time to say that he was no longer an agent, but intentionally not doing so. He knew Smithson knew he'd retired from the FBI and had addressed him as "Agent Warren" out of habit, but he thought he'd let the psychological edge, however minor, stand.

"I'm surprised to hear about your interest in our serial killer database. Wouldn't have expected we'd have a scrap of info that you're not already familiar with. Should I be flattered?"

"Well, sometimes it's not necessarily new information that

turns a key for you, but someone else's fresh insights into what you may have been looking at for so long that it's become stale."

"Ah, I see. So have we helped you?" Smithson asked.

"Indeed you have," Paul affirmed.

"Well, now I *am* flattered."

"Your people have been very thorough. Very impressive work."

"I have some very good investigative reporters."

"Yes you do. And it shows."

"I'll have to make sure they hear that you said so. But listen, I'd like to talk to you a little more about this in person, not that I'd imagine you'd be free to tell me what you're working on, but do you have plans for dinner?"

"Actually, I do have dinner plans, but I'd be happy to share with you *exactly* what I've been working on and I've only got maybe another hour or so of work to do here, so if you're in the building, why not just stop by? I can spare a half an hour or so."

"I'm not in the building, but I was planning to come down there before dinner, so yes, I'll do that. Say about five?"

"Five would be perfect."

"Okay then. See you in about an hour."

"See you then."

Both men hung up. Paul stood up, walked to the window and looked out at the city and the skyline. Smithson had played it cool and casual, but he'd gotten right to the point. Paul knew he could barely wait to hear his explanation of what he'd been looking for in GBC's files.

Paul returned to the desk and opened his attaché case. He opened the case that contained his 1911, removed the pistol, ejected the magazine and reinserted it, then chambered a round. He took the 1911's Alessi holster from the case and attached it to his belt over his right hip, then holstered the pistol. He then retrieved a small ankle holster from the attaché case and strapped it to his right ankle. Next he opened a small case that was attached to the inner side of the attaché case's lid and removed a Springfield Armory XD Sub Compact .40 automatic, checked its magazine, chambered a round and secured it in the ankle holster. He looked at the door to the hall. He knew Smithson would arrive a few minutes early. He sat back down at the desk, thought for a moment about calling Joan, but let the idea go just as quickly. He reached for the computer's mouse and resumed watching the show about Alexander Michael Dunlop.

116.

Whoever Speaks First Loses

The summer after Paul's freshman year in college, in order to earn some money for the next year of his school expenses, he briefly worked selling Flasharmor System home burglar alarms for a man named Solomon Rosenfield, who gave him his first training as a salesman.

Sol was born into a family of jewelers. He practically grew up in The Jeweler's Building in Cincinnati, Ohio and he was a born salesman. His grandfather had taught him that both men and women bought jewelry, but most of it was purchased by men *for* women, so one needed to present a product in a way that made the women feel they had to have it, then to explain how inexpensive the product was in comparison to one's competitor's products and to offer affordable financing that demonstrated how a low monthly payment made it seem that it would be shear folly not to purchase the product immediately and made the men appear to be not only fools but tightwads should they object to the purchase in any way. The next step was silence, to quietly await an agreement to buy the product, while being fully prepared to counter any objections.

Sol simply transferred this same technique to the selling of alarm systems. He found potential customers by offering a free home security analysis in newspaper advertisements and postcards mailed to the addresses of single family homes. When anyone responded, someone, one of his "cold callers", or often his salespeople themselves, would give them a call and attempt to arrange an appointment for a home security technician to visit their home to perform the free home security analysis. Sol stressed that couples were more likely to buy than single people. He told his staff that they should try to only make appointments with couples who *owned* their homes and to make the appointments only at times when both members of the couple would be there for the entire time of the analysis, which would take about forty-five minutes. The technician was, of course, a salesperson, who would examine the interior and exterior of the home while making notations on a clipboard chart, then sit with the homeowners and, after making further notations, explain to them the weak spots in their home's security. Then, while stressing the importance of protecting the family from home invaders, the salesperson would snap open his briefcase, which contained his demonstrator alarm system, and, without missing a beat, show how the clever Flasharmor unit reacted to the opening of the tiny door that was armed with it, by setting off an actual flashbulb. The flash was sensed by a sensor, which activated a loud bell.

"We mount the bell on the outside of your house and of course it will ring until you shut it off," the salesman would loudly say and he would then shut it off. Lowering his voice, placing the case aside and picking up his clipboard, he would then explain, "The beauty of the Flasharmor System is that it scares the burglar away immediately, effectively and cheaply. The flash startles him, he thinks his picture may have been taken and he's not going to stick around with that loud alarm bell alerting everyone in the neighborhood."

Turning the clipboard for the homeowners to view, he would then point out the home's identified weak spots, saying, "We install a Flasharmor unit at each door and window that a burglar might choose. A burglar will select the easiest and fastest way in and the way that appears to offer him the most protection from being seen.

He won't, for instance, climb to a second floor window facing the street, when he can more easily choose a first floor window or door, so, unless you insist, we need only install units on the doors and windows that are the potential weak spots, which helps make the entire system inexpensive." He would then carefully point to and count the weak spots on his chart and explain, "The units themselves require no wiring. The only hardwiring is from each sensor to the central control system, which is in turn wired to the bell. Some people like more than one bell, but in most cases one is sufficient."

Then, having already done the figuring and having written the details in clear, large print on a separate, simple contract page on his clipboard, he would then remove that page from the clipboard, and, while laying the contract and the chart of the weak spots on the table before the man say, "Now with W number of Flasharmor units and X number of sensors, we can protect your entire home and family for only Y dollars a month for 36 months or only Z dollars a month for 48 months. Would it be most convenient to have an installer here tomorrow night or would Saturday be better for you?"

"Now, after you've done that, whoever speaks first loses," Sol emphatically told Paul while training him.

"Really?" asked Paul.

"Absolutely. So you sit there and wait. You've pitched everything you've got. One or the other of 'em is going to answer your question and sign on the dotted line. Or they're going to ask for clarification and you've got 'em. You'll clarify whatever they need clarified. If they raise an objection to anything, you'll be prepared to counter any objection. If they ask if they can have 60 months to pay, you'll gladly give it to them, because it closes the deal, it makes their monthly payment so low that the guy looks like a putz if he's not willing to spend that much to protect his family and it costs them even more to finance for the longer period, so your commission is even bigger!"

Paul didn't sell Flasharmor Systems for a very long time, but he remembered what Sol had taught him about presenting his case and awaiting a reaction with complete confidence that whatever that reaction was, he would be able to turn it to his advantage.

He had in fact used the technique of "whoever speaks first loses" throughout his life in arguments, interviews and interrogations and had invariably found that once he'd made his pitch, as long as he had maintained his patience and his silence, if the other person had spoken, they'd eventually given him what he'd wanted.

Now, as it neared five o'clock in Vegas, Paul thought about Sol Rosenfield from Cincinnati and knew pretty well what he'd soon be saying to Phillip Smithson, how he'd be saying it and at just what point he'd be saying nothing.

117.

Confrontation

It surprised Paul that Smithson didn't arrive until exactly five o'clock, but he wasn't a moment late either. He knocked on the door and Paul bid him come in, rising from the desk and striding toward the door, which Smithson closed behind himself. Smithson was dressed in a sky blue golf shirt, khaki cargo pants and white Nike shoes. He was deeply tanned. They exchanged greetings, Smithson commenting on how Paul looked like retirement suited him and Paul replying that he was eating healthier, his wife being such a fine cook and all, and saying that he was exercising more, now that he had the time and since his diet now demanded it. Paul said that Smithson looked well, asked after his wife and expressed his condolences about the loss of their daughter. At this, for the first time since he'd entered the room, Smithson's smile faltered, but Paul noted that he continued to look him straight in the eye, like he was trying to read his thoughts, and that he never relaxed the two handed grip he had on Paul's right hand and wrist.

"We'll never get over losing her. She meant more to us than anything," he said.

"Of course," said Paul.

"Yes," Smithson simply said, nodding and momentarily biting his lower lip. Then, just as Paul was beginning to wonder what he might have to do to regain full possession of his right arm, Smithson finally released his grip, his eyes strayed to the computer monitor and he said, "So… I've got to tell you I'm awfully curious what our library might have had to offer you, Paul."

"Well, why don't you sit down," Paul gestured at the couch as he returned to the chair opposite the monitor, "and let me fill you in? It's a nearly incredible story really, but I think you'll appreciate it." He settled in the chair, leaned back with his elbows on its arms and interlaced his fingers looking across the desk at Smithson, who had sat on the couch and resumed his intent gaze into Paul's eyes.

"Steven Beck of Juneau, Alaska. Jerome Anthony of Santa Rosa, New Mexico. Kevin Pimental of New Bedford, Massachusetts. Arlen Henniford of Ogdensburg, New Jersey. Dennis Bordeaux of Buxton, Maine. And Daniel O'Reilly of Albany, New York. I'm sure you recognize the names," said Paul, noting all the while that Smithson had nodded at the mention of each name with a look in his eye that seemed to indicate both familiarity with the names and a growing interest in where Paul was leading.

"Of course," said Smithson with an emphasis and facial expression that said: *obviously; go on!*

"And of course you know they're all dead," said Paul, to which Smithson nodded vigorously and gestured just a bit with his hands as if to say: *so come on! What about it?*

"Well, the official stories on every one of them are that they all died accidentally or took their own lives. Pimental judged to be an accidental drug overdose, not a suicide. But the official stories are mistaken. They were all murdered," said Paul and he watched as Smithson didn't say a word, but leaned forward a bit, frowning and turning his head just enough to give the impression he wasn't quite sure he'd heard correctly and wanted his right ear to be directed more towards Paul. "What's more is that they were all murdered by the same person."

"And you think you've found him in our files!" Smithson blurted out with a tone of what sounded like genuine enthusiasm.

"No-o," said Paul in a manner that indicated that he thought Smithson ought to know better than to suggest such a thing and shook his head. "This isn't someone who's ever likely to be in your files."

He looked at Smithson and waited. Finally Smithson raised his palms and made a face as if to say: *well?*

"But I know who he is," Paul continued. "He's a man with a special forces background, a trained killer with an axe to grind. He's made a lifetime study of serial killers and finally something snapped in him and he decided to start executing them."

"Now wait a minute," said Smithson, holding up his right hand. "I'm not saying you're wrong, but let me play devil's advocate for a minute. Weren't all the causes of death different with each of these guys? Wouldn't that indicate completely different M.O.s?"

Now Paul thought Smithson had shown just the tiniest chink in his armor and he replied, "Not necessarily. First of all, this guy's not so pathological that he's married to a method of killing and he's an expert at killing in maybe a hundred or more ways. Secondly, what was important was that the deaths all were made to look like accidents or suicides. That's his real M.O. Also, the four that weren't already associated with their victims were intentionally left dead among evidence of their victims. And the clincher? The nooses used for the two hangings were identically fashioned. Different materials. Exactly the same knots."

Smithson nodded, but he didn't say a word. He rested his left elbow on his right wrist, rubbed his chin between the thumb and index finger of his left hand and just sat there looking Paul in the eye, appearing very much to be pondering what he'd just been told.

Minutes passed. Finally Smithson asked, "You took your law degree at Notre Dame, didn't you?"

Paul nodded.

"Good school," commented Smithson. He smiled slightly. He took a deep breath. "No doubt you could have made a very good living as a lawyer, but instead you chose to join the FBI. Almost thirty odd years of chasing bad guys and then you retire at fifty-five after the Johansen case took the wind out of your sails."

Now Paul looked like he was the one who hadn't heard correctly.

"I'm not blaming you, Paul. Not in the slightest. Really. How could any of us have been the same after that? But that's my point. I don't pretend to know exactly what you were thinking, but you were all done and you knew it, so you retired.

"And again you probably could have gone on to make a good living as a lawyer, but prosecution is for young hotshots trying to make a name for themselves, and defense?... well, let's face it, defense is defense of bad guys, right? So what do you do? You decide to be a consultant, an expert witness, and you select cases in which you can testify and hammer home sterling evidence for the winning side of the case."

Now they sat opposite each other, silently. Smithson wasn't sure if he'd expected a reaction. Paul saw no need to give him one and was simply waiting for him to go on.

Finally he did.

"Again, I don't blame you at all, Paul. If we all learned anything from Johansen's being set free, it's that the system is broken, so who can blame you for only getting involved when you can stack the deck?"

Paul nodded once, as if to concede the point.

"This guy sounds like you, except where he's seen the deck's been stacked in favor of the wrong side, he's stepped up and reshuffled it and dealt a new hand. Like you, he's made sure that the people who should lose *do* lose.

"You say you know who this guy is. You mean you've profiled him. You know the exact type that he is. Or do you mean you know just exactly who he is, that you have proof of who he is?"

Paul was studying Smithson's body language. He'd been examining the lines and the fit of his clothing all along and believed he was unarmed, not that he thought for a moment that Smithson needed a weapon to be deadly.

Paul answered, "Do I have proof of who he is? No, I can't say I do." At this he saw Smithson markedly relax. "In some instances I don't know just how he figured out what he certainly did figure out or exactly how he did what he definitely did, but I know this: I know he's a man who, when he learned that his real mother was his parents' former French maid, was never the same person as he'd been before. I know that when his father cut off the woman's stipend, believing she had betrayed their secret in a letter she wrote him from Marseilles when he graduated from high school, she was left to die in poverty of a heroin overdose. I know that when he learned of her death his hatred of his father became an urge to kill so great that he went to war so that he *could* kill with impunity. I know this guy thinks he's a hero."

Smithson had been visibly stunned at the mention of his mother, but he now said, "But you don't think so."

"What I *know* is that even though this guy has studied serial killers since he was a boy, he doesn't realize that he's a serial killer now himself. Worse yet, he doesn't understand that it's an addiction and that he probably can't stop." Paul stood up, picked up his attaché case from the desk and began to move toward the door, never taking his eyes off Smithson's. "However, he'd better stop, because, although I have no absolute proof that he's done what he has done, I know who he is and if he keeps doing it, I'll eventually have enough evidence that I'll be forced to do something about it."

With that Paul opened the door and began to step into the hall, then he turned to Smithson again and said, "And by the way, if he goes down, his best friend is going with him as an accessory to some of, if not all six of the murders." Then he stepped out, closed the door behind himself and walked down the hall.

118.

Crocodiles

Smithson sat on the couch looking at the office door, stroking his chin and thinking about what he'd just been told. He glanced at the back of the computer monitor, the top of the desk, the counter, the coffeemaker, the cabinets and around the whole room. After a while he stood up, walked to the window, rested his fingertips on the windowsill and surveyed the Las Vegas cityscape without a thought about what he was viewing.

Eventually, an airliner that had just taken off caught his eye and, as it climbed into the sky and flew west, he watched it until it was no longer visible. He checked the time on his wristwatch, then took his cell phone from his pocket, opened it to his contact list, scrolled down, selected a name, placed a call and looked out at the sky to the west, where the plane had disappeared, as he listened to the ringing on his phone.

"Hey Bird, how y' doin'?... Never better, thanks. Say, where are you?... Good. Y' get it fixed?... Yeah, of course. I might've known better than to ask... So I'm guessing you haven't had dinner yet if you've been wrestling with an engine all afternoon... I don't really care; whatever and wherever you like. I'm not really all that hungry; I just want to pow-wow... Joe's in half an hour is perfect... Sure, I can give you more than a hint; my phone's not bugged; is your's?... No reason; I'm kidding, Bird... Yeah, I s'pose you're right; sorry... So anyways, you got over to Australia from Nam a time or two for R&R, didn't you?... No, I never did, but I'm thinkin' I might like to go there now and hunt some crocodiles. What d' y' think? You want to take a little trip down under?"

About the Author

Bob Druwing is perhaps best known as a movie and TV actor. He is also a singer-songwriter, cartoonist and fine artist. After 50 years of insufficient practice, he insists that he plays guitar as well as any novice. As of this writing, he is "in talks" regarding production of his first screenplay: *Rate Of Recovery*. He keeps homes in Los Angeles, Maine and Massachusetts. *He Could Have Done Anything* is his first novel.